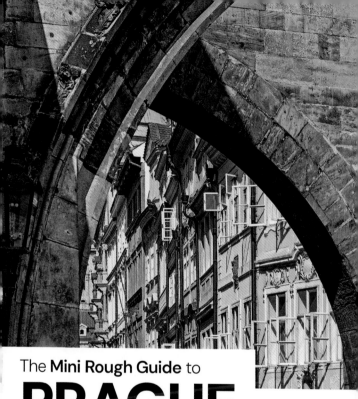

The **Mini Rough Guide** to
PRAGUE

T0321214

ROUGH GUIDES

YOUR TAILOR-MADE TRIP
STARTS HERE

Tailor-made trips and unique adventures crafted by local experts

HOW ROUGHGUIDES.COM/TRIPS WORKS

STEP 1

Pick your dream destination, tell us what you want and submit an enquiry.

STEP 2

Fill in a short form to tell your local expert about yo[ur] dream trip and preference[s]

STEP 3

Our local expert will craft your tailor-made itinerary. You'll be able to tweak and refine it until you're completely satisfied.

STEP 4

Book online with ease, pa[ck] your bags and enjoy the trip! Our local expert will b[e] on hand 24/7 while you're on the road.

PLAN AND BOOK YOUR TRIP AT
ROUGHGUIDES.COM/TRIPS

How to download your Free eBook

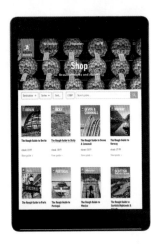

1. Visit **www.roughguides.com/ free-ebook** or scan the **QR code** opposite

2. Enter the code **prague514**

3. Follow the simple step-by-step instructions

For troubleshooting contact: mail@roughguides.com

Contents

Introduction

Located in the heart of Europe, Prague (*Praha* in Czech) on the banks of the Vltava River has become one of the world's premier tourist destinations. Known primarily for its architecture, beer, nightlife and cultural offerings, the Czech capital draws almost eight million visitors a year.

Some cities still have the capacity to stop even the most hardened traveller in their tracks, and Prague is one of them. Never destroyed by war, the city's 1000-year history is etched into

WHAT'S NEW

Despite its status as a leading city break destination, the Czech capital refuses to sit still: in among all its history swirl fresh ideas and a thriving food and cultural scene. *Mandarin Oriental, Prague* has created a major new dining experience in monastery turned restaurant *Monastiq* (see page 127), paying homage to traditional cuisine through gourmet twists on Czech classics. The biggest new hotel to open for some time in the city centre is *Cloud One Prague* (Hybernská 17; www.the-cloud-one.com), which is crowned by a rooftop terrace offering great views of the historic core. Prague City Tourism has launched new tours of the Clementinum building (see page 63) offering visitors access to never-seen-before spaces such as the Baroque library, the astronomical tower and the meridian hall; book via the website (www.prague.eu). Getting around is now easier than ever with one-day motorway e-vignettes available for 200Kč (see page 135) – perfect for those embarking on a day-trip from the capital by car. Trolleybuses have also made a comeback in the capital after an absence of over five decades, replacing the buses that run to the airport from Nádraží Veleslavín metro station in 2024 (see page 130). Prague Airport, now fully recovered from the global Covid-19 pandemic, is also busy adding new flights to places no airline has ever served from the Czech capital, such as the Azores and Mongolia.

A sea of red roofs in central Prague

its very fabric, its sublime beauty and unique character forged through its emergence as a major European hub. It has been the capital of Bohemia for centuries and is now the epicentre of an increasingly confident Czech Republic.

During the Middle Ages it rose to prominence as the capital of Charles IV (1316–78), the Holy Roman Emperor and ruler of much of Western Europe. In the late sixteenth and early seventeenth centuries the city was the seat of the Habsburg Court, and it became the capital of the newly independent country of Czechoslovakia in 1918.

The Communists took over in 1948, but they were overthrown in the Prague-based Velvet Revolution of 1989. And when the Czechs and Slovaks parted company in 1992, Prague became capital of the new country that was formed.

THE VLTAVA

As Prague's architecture envelops you in all its glory, you could be forgiven for overlooking one of the city's most beautiful sights: the Vltava itself, its graceful S-shape waterway threading through the heart of the city. At times going under its German name of Moldau, for centuries it has inspired writers and musicians alike, notably Bedřich Smetana whose symphonic poem dedicated to the river celebrates its lengthy journey across the Czech landscape on its way to Prague.

Prague always was, and still is, a city of contrasts. It is famous for its illustrious artistic past and present – in painting, sculpture, music, literature, architecture and design – yet is equally renowned for its beer, filling food and oversubscribed tourist scene. Prague is also a place of protest and revolution, asserting its own identity, from the fifteenth-century Hussites who fought against the hegemony of the Catholic Church, to the struggle against Communist domination in 1968 and, more successfully, 1989. This is also a city that has completely embraced consumerism, with big, brash shopping centres springing up across its streets. Nightlife is also a huge draw, from highbrow classical music to the bustling pubs popular for their cheap beer. All these factors mean Prague attracts a very mixed crowd. It has something for just about everyone, apart from beach lovers.

CITY OF A HUNDRED SPIRES

Prague's architectural tapestry spans almost every major European style, with extraordinary examples of Romanesque, Gothic, Renaissance, Baroque, Art Nouveau and Modernist design interwoven across the city. The facades showcase the work of master painters and sculptors, and behind them have played some of Europe's finest musicians, including Mozart, Dvořák and Smetana. Also part of the fabric are the threads of political and religious intrigue.

Pride of place must go to Prague Castle, the seat of royal power throughout the Middle Ages. It sits on the top of a low ridge, casting a watchful eye over the city. Royal patronage spawned a court, which in turn drew the rich and powerful. These families spent fortunes building extravagant mansions and summer palaces using the top craftspeople of their time.

The Church also played its part, but the situation was complicated: Bohemia at this time represented a major battleground between partisans of Catholicism and church reformers. The many impressive cathedrals, churches, chapels, convents and monasteries attest to the ferocity of the struggle – and the eventual triumph of the Catholic Church – and have given Prague the nickname 'city of a hundred spires'.

Prague Castle's guarded gates

These waves of building and rebuilding have created one of Europe's most impressive cityscapes. Although there is no doubt that Prague looks beautiful on a bright summer's day, it is equally enchanting framed by the copper tints of autumn or blanketed by crisp winter snow. Seen at night, it is no less disappointing, with reflections on the Vltava and the buildings highlighted in the waxy glow of streetlights.

ART, CULTURE AND LEISURE

Centuries of music, theatre and art have nurtured a cultured and urbane society: the people of Prague appreciate their theatres and galleries as much as visitors do, revelling in the artistic legacy of the Habsburg years and the flourish of artistic endeavours that

Charles Bridge attracts many visitors

┌─ **WHEN TO GO** ──────────────────────────────

Prague is a year-round destination, though some months are better than others – and not just because of the weather. Hordes of tourists descend on the city in the summer and for the Christmas markets, so to avoid the crowds, visit in late spring or mid-autumn. The quietest months are November and February but be aware that winters in the Czech Republic are bitterly cold. It's best to avoid a visit in Easter when many businesses close. If you are planning to visit castles and other sights outside the capital, be aware that many are not open year-round, often closing from late autumn to Easter.

└───

accompanied the growing nationalism of the nineteenth century. Ticket prices for concerts and other performances in the city are still very reasonable compared to Western Europe and allow locals and visitors from all walks of life the chance to enjoy Prague's rich culture.

However, culture doesn't have to mean highbrow. The Czech Republic is one of the world's leading beer producers, and people are just as at home sipping a few drinks in the city's numerous beer halls or spending the evening at a dimly lit jazz club or rock bar. The café society that nurtured many of the Prague's artists, from Kafka to Havel, still survives in pockets of the city, especially in traditional haunts like *Slavia* and *Louvre*, but most places these days have been given over to beer consumption for the arriving masses.

THE MODERN CITY

There have been many changes since 1989 for both the capital and its people to say the least. The younger generations now grow up with the freedom long taken for granted by most in the West and in many ways, Prague is little different from any other large European city. The streets are now full of the international clothing you see in the likes of London, Paris and Milan. People stare at their smartphone on the metro, music is dominated by the same names you encounter elsewhere, and locals likely watch the same TV series as you do, though probably dubbed into Czech.

SUSTAINABLE TRAVEL

Prague suffers from overtourism, but there are things conscientious travellers can do to help soothe the city's woes. Short-term rentals make up a large sector of the accommodation in Prague but have turned whole pockets of the city into ghost towns, key safes bristling from every lamppost. Very often, these central apartments are owned by foreigners and none of your money stays in the city. Booking direct with small, Czech-owned guesthouses and hotels is a more sustainable way to stay.

One of the worst aspects of short-term rentals is a disregard from guests for social etiquette and behaviour; the Czech Republic has strict noise restrictions between 10pm and 7am, a rule that's generally well observed by residents but often broken by tourists. You should also be aware that consuming alcohol in public, including tenement block stairwells and yards, is banned – though some tourists seem to regard the city as one big beer garden. Remember, the city is home to a working community, it is not your playground.

Matrioshka dolls, Soviet military badges, cannabis lollipops, hookah pipes, Polish vodka, fake Borussia Dortmund football shirts… the list of 'typical' Prague souvenirs is as long as it is touristy (and often downright offensive or illegal). Try to source Czech-made mementos of your trip from independent shops that stock the work of local artisans, such as *Botanicus*, *Manufaktura*, and *Orel and friends* in Malá Strana. Certainly, avoid the touristy souvenir shops that tout for business along the Royal Route, especially those found in Karlova.

Finally, Prague has one of the planet's best public transport systems – use it! It's cheap, reliable and efficient, and keeps you off Prague's clogged-up roads.

Prague's historic core is a UNESCO World Heritage Site

The historic centre of Prague was listed by UNESCO as a World Heritage Site in the early 1990s, which has thankfully protected the architecturally rich core from development. Many old buildings have been restored to their original glory after decades of neglect, though sadly not all the renovations have been sensitive or preserved the authenticity of the buildings. Parts of the city outside the boundaries of the UNESCO-conserved site have been sacrificed to glass and steel.

The beauty of this city is also its downfall. It is near-impossible to visit Prague and dodge fellow travellers, from honeymooning couples to budget-conscious students and large tour groups. And yet Prague remains one of Europe's most alluring and fascinating places to explore, with peaceful corners, or even whole districts, ripe for discovery by those willing to make the effort.

10 Things not to miss

A perfect day in
Prague

9AM

Breakfast. Kickstart your day with a coffee at the charming *Cukrkávalimonáda* café (Lázeňská 7) in the Lesser Quarter. See page 125.

10AM

Church of St Nicholas. Just around the corner, on Malostranské Square, is the Church of St Nicholas, a Lesser Quarter landmark. This has one of the finest Baroque interiors in the city, glittering with gold leaf. See page 53.

11AM

Fine views. From Malostranské Square make your way up steep Nerudova Street, lined with historic buildings, and climb up the ramp of Ke Hradu to Hradčany Square. From here take in the wonderful view across the city's domes and spires. See page 36.

NOON

Nový Svět and lunch. Close to Hradčany Square is the delightful Nový Svět neighbourhood. At the very end of the street that runs through the district you'll find the timber *Hotel U Raka* which has a quaint rural feel. Grab a table at the small on-site café for a light lunch of *polévka* (soup) and *chlebíčky* (open sandwiches). See page 127.

2PM

Castle tour. Head back to Hradčany Square and duck inside the castle gate. Spend the afternoon exploring St Vitus Cathedral, peeping inside the

beautifully decorated Wenceslas Chapel, and browsing the historic rooms of the Old Palace and the medieval Vladislav Hall. See page 41.

4PM

Formal gardens. Once you've had your fill of palatial grandeur, walk to the formal Baroque gardens that cascade down the hill beneath Prague Castle, returning to the Lesser Quarter via Valdštejnské Square. See page 49.

5PM

Charles Bridge. Amble along Tomašská back to Malostranské Square where Mostecká will lead down to the Charles Bridge. Soak up the serene views of the river and castle hill. As the sun goes down, catch the last rays in Kampa Park beneath the arches of the Gothic bridge. See page 57.

7PM

Dinner. When it comes to dining, there are a number of excellent options close by to choose from. *U Modré kachničky* (see page 127) is a cosy, romantic bolthole, while *Kampa Park* (see page 126) pairs Vltava views and excellent cuisine.

9.30PM

On the town. Soak up the magic of the Old Town at night by crossing Charles Bridge and taking Karlova to the Old Town Square. Round off the evening with a cocktail – try *Cloud 9* (Pobřežní 1), *Bugsy's* (Pařížská 10), *Ocean Drive* (V Kolkovně 7) or *Tretter's* (V Kolkovně 3). See page 100.

Communist
Prague

9AM

Breakfast. Bypass the opulent hotel breakfast buffet in favour of a more suitable spartan affair. Head to *Havelská Koruna* for a plate of pancakes or a pair of sausages washed down with a mug of strong Turkish coffee. See page 122.

10AM

Museum of Communism. Strike out along Na Příkopě to Náměstí republiky, swinging by the excellent Museum of Communism for an insight into life in Czechoslovakia under Soviet rule. Various mock-ups of interiors contain period objects. Most disturbing are the sections on the secret police and the Iron Curtain. Allow at least two hours to see everything. See page 73.

1PM

People's Canteen. For lunch, head along Na Poříčí to Těšnov where *Lidová Jídelna* transports diners back to the days of the socialist utopia. Prices here are some of the lowest you'll find in the city. See page 126.

2PM

Velvet Revolution Memorial. Take the city's very communist-era metro (mostly built in the 1970s and 1980s) from Florenc to Národní třída. At Národní třída 16, you'll find the Velvet Revolution Monument, a series of hands giving the 'V for victory' sign. It was here on Národní třída that protesting students were attacked by riot police on 17 November 1989, sparking the Velvet Revolution that finally ended forty years of communism in Czechoslovakia.

3PM

Secret Police Street. Around the corner is Bartolomějská Street where the secret police headquarters were located during the communist era. This is where dissidents were brought for interrogation and worse. Many of the facades still look the same as they did in the late 1980s.

4PM

Retro Museum. Until 2024, Prague's superb Retro Museum was set within the most communist of all the city's department stores, Kotva. However, restoration work on the shopping centre has forced the museum to move. The unrivalled collection of consumer items from the days of the socialist republic is looking for a new permanent home, but should it have found one by the time of your trip, it's a must-visit.

7PM

Dinner. It's time to return to the twenty-first century. Make a beeline for the raucous *Červený Jelen* (see page 121), located near Masarykovo railway station, for traditional Bohemian meat dishes, washed down with a pint of beer. For a more sedate, meat-free evening, try the excellent vegetarian restaurant *Lehká Hlava* (see page 123).

Prague on a
budget

8AM

Breakfast. Most hotels in Prague include breakfast in their rates and are known for laying on rich spreads – so fill up while you can. Otherwise, there are plenty of café-bakeries (*cukrárna*) where you can buy a pastry and a coffee for under 100Kč. Try *Svatováclavská cukrárn* (see page 124) or *U Knoflíčků* (see page 127).

9AM

Cross the Vltava. You don't have to pay a single crown to see one of Prague's biggest attractions – Charles Bridge. You can peruse the statues along its balustrade, take photos of the Gothic panorama, with Prague Castle rising in the background, and wander the cobblestones without opening your wallet. See page 57.

10AM

Lennon and Kampa. From Charles Bridge, head down the steps near the Malá Strana end to reach Kampa Island. The pretty square and parkland can be explored for free, and you can feed the resident swans. Just off Kampa, on Velkopřevorské náměstí is the famous Lennon Wall, one of Eastern Europe's most-visited pieces of graffiti. See page 56.

11AM

Tram No 22. This tramline swings by many of the city's sights including Prague Castle, the National Theatre, Charles Square, Malostranské náměstí and several others. Fashion your own ninety-minute hop-on, hop-off sightseeing tour for just 40Kč, boarding at Hellichova near the Lennon Wall. This tram is very popular with tourists so be careful of pickpockets.

1PM

Lunch specials. Wherever you choose to hop off tram No 22, you are bound to find a restaurant offering a cheap lunch special. All Czech eateries churn out inexpensive set meals for locals whose workplace doesn't have its own canteen; here you can order a two-course lunch for under 200Kč. Otherwise, most supermarkets offer ready-made dishes and picnic supplies for affordable prices.

2.30PM

Prague hike. Very few visitors to Prague know that you can walk in pretty countryside without leaving the city limits. Jump off tram No 22 at Malostranské náměstí and change onto tram No 20 to Divoká Šárka. From here, a red-marked Czech Hiking Club trail runs 7.5km to Baba on the Vltava. This is an easy walk along the Šárecké Valley with its rock formations and forests. The Czech map app Mapy.cz will guide you through the gorge (and the rest of the city for that matter). After, catch tram No 8 or No 18 back to the centre.

7PM

Cheap dinners. After a long day, you've earned a good dinner. For reasonable prices, grab a meal at *Lokal Dlouháááá* (see page 123) or *Mincovna* (see page 124).

History

More than most peoples, the Czechs are aware of the history that has moulded them, and which continues to affect their present and influence their future. In its present form as an independent democratic republic, their country has existed only since 1993; before that, as a small nation, they were more often than not subjected to interference and domination by larger and more powerful neighbours.

BEGINNINGS

Located at a natural ford on the Vltava River, a tributary of the Elbe River, Prague was inhabited as early as the Stone Age, and remains including tools and jewels have been unearthed in the area. Celtic tribes settled here well over two thousand years ago, followed by Germanic peoples. Of more lasting significance, however, was the arrival in the fifth or sixth century AD of the first Slavs, ancestors of the Czechs, who settled here. The second half of the ninth century saw the construction of the castle's original fortifications. It was from here that the Czechs were ruled by the Přemyslid family, a dynasty with mythical roots.

NOTES

The Czech national myth goes that Princess Libuše, leader of a Slavonic matriarchal tribe, picked the farmer Přemysl to be her husband. She told him to go look for a village on the banks of the Vltava and to found a town there, which she predicted would achieve great things. This later became Prague, the 'golden city'.

A SAINTLY PIONEER

In the late ninth century, the Greek missionaries Cyril and Methodius brought Christianity to the Slavic lands. In around 873, Methodius baptised Prince Bořivoj and his wife Ludmila. Cyril and Methodius went on to be canonised, as did Ludmila, proclaimed patron saint of Bohemia following her assassination. The grandson of Ludmila, first of the rulers named Wenceslas (Václav in Czech), held the crown in the tenth century. During his reign, a church dedicated to St Vitus was built at Prague Castle. Wenceslas, who was a fervent believer, became the first of the Czech princes to be murdered while carrying out his holy duties. He was ambushed on his way to Mass by his younger brother, Boleslav.

King Wenceslas

Far from being condemned for eliminating Wenceslas, Boleslav assumed power. During his reign, a well-travelled Jewish merchant by the name of Ibrahim ibn Jacob wrote admiringly of Prague as a great and busy trading centre with solid stone buildings. The town became a bishopric in 973, at about the time that the monastery of St George was established.

In the early eleventh century, Přemyslid rule was extended to neighbouring Moravia by Břetislav I, the great-grandson of Boleslav. He later became a vassal of the German emperor, paving the way for centuries of German influence. Břetislav's son, Vratislav II, was the first monarch to bear the title of King of Bohemia.

PŘEMYSLID HEYDAY

Arguably the greatest of the Přemyslid rulers was Otakar II (1230–78), known as the 'King of Gold and Iron' for his prowess in war and the prosperity he brought the kingdom. Otakar encouraged German merchants, miners and craftspeople to settle in Bohemia and he founded the Lesser Quarter as a German enclave, protected by German law. His ambitions were abruptly thwarted when he was slain in battle by his Austrian rival for the imperial throne, Rudolf of Habsburg, but under Wenceslas II, Otakar's son, the economy boomed. Thanks to silver mining, the Prague groschen became a stable international currency.

The dynasty's luck eventually ran out with the son of Wenceslas II. In the summer of 1306, early in his reign, the teenage King Wenceslas III went down in history as the last of the Přemyslid kings when he was assassinated in Moravia.

BOHEMIA UNDER CHARLES IV

The Přemyslid dynasty was succeeded by the House of Luxembourg. The first ruler was John (Jan) of Luxembourg, but it was his son Charles IV (Karel IV) who became the best-known Czech king. Ruling for 36 years, Charles was deeply involved in the government of Prague and Bohemia. His good relations with the Vatican led to Prague being promoted to an archbishopric in 1344. Under his direction, centuries of work began on the present St Vitus Cathedral.

Early in his reign in 1348, Charles put Prague firmly on the intellectual map by founding Central Europe's first university. He expanded the city to the New Town and started work on Charles Bridge. In 1355, Charles was crowned Holy Roman Emperor.

RELIGIOUS STRIFE

Prague should have thrived as the administrative headquarters of the empire that Charles had consolidated, but events conspired against it. Charles IV's son and successor, Wenceslas IV, proved an incompetent ruler. He turned his back on revolts and wars and was eventually deposed. In the biggest crisis that Wenceslas failed

The mosaic of the Last Judgement adorns St Vitus Cathedral

to address, Prague lived through the violent outbreaks that were preludes to the Reformation. At the Bethlehem Chapel, in the Old Town, a theologian and professor named Jan Hus challenged the excesses of the Catholic Church. Hus's demands for reform became so vigorous that he was excommunicated, arrested for heresy and burnt at the stake in Konstanz in 1415. The Hussite Movement was born, much to the dismay of the papacy.

THE FIRST DEFENESTRATION

In 1419 a reformist mob invaded Prague's New Town Hall, liberated imprisoned Hussites and threw several Catholic city councillors from the windows. This event, called the First Defenestration of Prague, was to herald an odd tradition. The harried brother of the unfortunate Wenceslas, Emperor Sigismund, marshalled Czech

Catholic forces and foreign allies in a crusade against the Hussites. However, the rebels fought back. Their underequipped, but highly motivated, peasant army won some major victories, such as at the Battle of Vítkov Hill. The rebels were commanded by a brilliant one-eyed soldier named Jan Žižka (after which the Prague neighbourhood of Žižkov is named), but following his death the leadership foundered, and they were eventually defeated.

Sigismund died without leaving a successor. He was followed by the short-lived reigns of his son-in-law Albrecht of Austria, and then of Albrecht's son, Ladislas. A dynamic politician by the name of George of Poděbrady, who was implicated in the death of Ladislas, was elected to succeed him. George aligned himself with the Hussites, to the displeasure of the neighbouring Catholic kings and the papacy. He was eventually excommunicated and, along with Prague, boycotted by the international diplomatic and business community.

ARRIVAL OF THE HABSBURGS

Absentee kings ruled Bohemia from George's death until 1526, when the Habsburgs claimed the throne. This zealously Catholic dynasty held sway over what remained of the Holy Roman Empire and focused their attention on protecting their European borders against the very real Ottoman threat. By now the Protestant faith had become a powerful influence, in addition to which Bohemia's grave religious divisions were simply another thorn in their side.

In 1576 Emperor Rudolph II came to the throne and moved his capital from Vienna to Prague. Imperial

> **NOTES**
>
> Rudolph II (1583–1611), Prague's emperor under the Renaissance, was fascinated by the occult. He employed a number of alchemists, including Englishman Edward Kelley who was later imprisoned at Křivoklát Castle.

Prague's National Theatre, symbol of Czech national pride

patronage spurred the arts and sciences to new heights, and splendid Renaissance buildings further embellished the city. Rudolph's principal accomplishment was a decree granting freedom of religion to Catholics and Protestants alike. However, the decree was not honoured by Ferdinand II, the Catholic king who succeeded him in 1611, and the inherent religious conflict soon escalated.

Another defenestration in 1618 was the starting shot for the disastrous Thirty Years War. A new king, Frederick of the Palatinate, was elected, but in 1620 his Protestant army was routed by the imperial forces on a low hill just outside Prague. What became known as the Battle of White Mountain has gone down as one of the blackest days in Czech history; its aftermath was marked by the public execution of leading Protestants and the expulsion from the country of all those who refused to convert to Catholicism.

Ferdinand's decisive victory radically changed the face of Prague. The period that followed was a time when Czechs were a suppressed majority in their own land, their elite either dead or in exile, their language downgraded, and their religion forbidden. Confiscated Protestant estates were sold at knock-down prices to Habsburg supporters, many of them foreigners. German became the language of polite society, and Czech was eventually spoken only by peasants and the urban poor. Jesuits and other religious orders strove to eliminate the last sparks of Protestantism. However, not all was gloom. Once the country had recovered from the decades of war, a building boom beautified cities and countryside with sugary Baroque art and architecture.

NATIONAL AWAKENING

In the eighteenth century, Habsburg rule became more enlightened, notably in the reign of Empress Maria Theresa (1740–1780). Her educational reforms produced a generation of literate Czechs, who became increasingly aware of their past history and their present subjugation. In the early nineteenth century, a new intellectual

THE SECOND DEFENESTRATION

Cornered in Prague Castle by their angry Protestant adversaries on 23 May 1618, two terrified imperial officials begged for mercy, but their pleas went unheeded. Bundled to the window along with their unfortunate secretary, they were forced out, though one of them clung desperately to the sill until his knuckles were broken by a sharp blow from a dagger. Their descent into the moat far below should have killed them, but to everyone's surprise, they survived the fall, and succeeded in making their escape. According to the Catholic version of the event, they were miraculously borne up by the Virgin Mary; the possibly more realistic Protestant account describes how their fall was broken by the monstrous mound of rubbish that had accumulated in the moat.

elite emerged, codifying the Czech language, reviving its literature and agitating for Czech rights within the Empire. By the end of the century, Prague had been reverted to a Czech city with buildings like the National Museum and National Theatre expressing a confident Czech nationalism.

The statue of Jan Hus gazes out over Old Town Square

THE TWENTIETH CENTURY

When the heir to the Habsburg throne, Archduke Franz Ferdinand, was assassinated in June 1914, the Austro-Hungarian Empire was plunged into World War I. From the ashes of a defeated Austria-Hungary, an independent Czechoslovak republic was proclaimed in October 1918, comprising Bohemia, Moravia, Slovakia and Ruthenia. The first president of the First Republic was Tomáš G. Masaryk, a professor of philosophy.

WORLD WAR II AND AFTER

However, simmering tensions between the Czech and Slovak majority and the country's sizable German minority came to a head when, in 1938, Hitler demanded self-determination for Czechoslovakia's German-speaking citizens in the Sudetenland. In order to appease him, Britain and France handed over these border regions. In March 1939, after persuading Slovak nationalists to secede and form an ostensibly independent, near-Fascist 'Slovak State', Hitler created the

Memorial to the Victims of Communism

'Protectorate of Bohemia-Moravia'. Six long years of brutal occupation were to follow before Soviet troops liberated the city in May 1945.

At the parliamentary elections of 1946, the communists won nearly forty percent of the votes. The non-communist pre-war president Edvard Beneš, elected again, invited the veteran communist leader Klement Gottwald to form a coalition cabinet. When, in 1948, several non-communist ministers resigned in protest at his policies, Gottwald packed the government with supporters. When the very popular non-communist Foreign Minister Jan Masaryk, son of Tomáš, was found dead below his office window at the foreign ministry it was whispered that he was the victim of another defenestration.

Gottwald, as the new president, framed a five-year economic plan, cracked down on the church and purged his opponents outside and inside the party; scores were executed, and thousands arrested. The show trials went on under Antonín Novotný, while farmers were forced into collectives.

The short-lived Prague Spring of 1968 saw an attempt by reform communists led by the Slovak Alexander Dubček to transform the system and create 'socialism with a human face'. This failed, crushed by the Soviet tanks which overran the country in August. For the next two decades, reinstated hardline communists ruled the roost, buying off the populace by filling the shop shelves with consumer goods. The few dissidents, among them playwright Václav Havel, suffered routine harassment, persecution and imprisonment.

THE CZECH REPUBLIC

In November 1989 the so-called Velvet Revolution saw Václav Havel elected as president, an office he was to hold for thirteen years. While successive governments struggled with the problems of converting the communist system into a free-market economy, Havel fought for the survival of the country whose freedom he had suffered for. In vain: in 1992, the Czech prime minister Václav Klaus and nationalist Slovak leader Vladimír Mečiar engineered the Velvet Divorce, the creation of separate Czech and Slovak Republics.

The disappointed Havel submitted himself to re-election as president of his now-diminished country, finally being replaced by

THE VELVET REVOLUTION

On 17 November 1989, an event took place that should have been a peaceful student demonstration but turned into a mass movement after police attempted to quell the event by beating protesters. Thousands then gathered on Wenceslas Square to call for the introduction of democracy, rattling their house keys as a symbol of protest against forty years of communism. The regime eventually stepped down and Havel became president after what became known as the Velvet Revolution.

Václav Havel memorial, 2011

Klaus in 2003. Despite setbacks, the Czech Republic has steadily integrated itself into the political and economic systems of the West. Membership of NATO came in 1999, and in 2004 the country joined the European Union (EU).

Since joining the EU, the Czech Republic has largely prospered and now enjoys a standard of living equal to the European average in most areas of life. However, corruption, political instability and often shocking populism still taint Eastern Europe's most successful country. Prague has become almost a Western capital though it suffers from overtourism and overcrowding. The war in Ukraine has had a significant effect on the city, with hundreds of thousands of Ukrainian refugees now living and working in Prague.

CHRONOLOGY

c.400 BC Invasion by a Celtic tribe, the Boii, who give Bohemia its name.

AD 400 Arrival of the Slavs.

900–1306 Rule of the Přemyslid dynasty; building of Prague Castle.

1306 Assassination of the young King Wenceslas II and end of the Přemyslid dynasty.

1344 Prague becomes an archbishopric.

1348–78 Reign of Charles IV; building of Charles Bridge.

1398–1415 Jan Hus preaches religious reform and is burnt at the stake.

1420–1526 Hussite Wars.

1576 Prague becomes capital of the Habsburg Empire.

1609 Decree granting religious freedom.

1618 Decree revoked by Ferdinand II. Thirty Years' War ensues.

1620 Catholic victory at Battle of the White Mountain. Repressive measures against Protestants resulting in large-scale exile.

1787 Première of Mozart's Don Giovanni.

1918 Independent Republic of Czechoslovakia proclaimed.

1938 Munich Agreement cedes the Sudetenland to Hitler.

1939–45 Nazi invasion and occupation.

1945 Prague liberated by the Resistance and the Red Army.

1948 Communist coup d'état.

1968 Prague Spring.

1989 Velvet Revolution. Václav Havel elected president.

1993 'Velvet Divorce' separates Czech and Slovak republics.

1999 NATO accession.

2004 The Czech Republic joins the EU.

2008 A controversial agreement signed to locate US anti-missile defences on Czech soil.

2009 The centre-right government of Mirek Topolanek falls.

2011 Václav Havel dies, a three-day national mourning is declared.

2013 Miloš Zeman elected president, corruption scandal leads to political turmoil and early elections.

2020 The Covid-19 global pandemic shuts down Prague.

2022 Refugees flood into Prague after Russia launches a full-scale invasion of Ukraine.

2023 Former NATO general Petr Pavel is sworn in as the fourth president of the Czech Republic.

2024 At the Paris Olympics, tennis players Tomáš Macháč and Kateřina Siniaková win gold in the mixed doubles; the Czech fencing team secure a surprising bronze.

The river-threaded Czech capital

Places

Prague is without doubt one of the most spectacular cities to visit in the world. Almost every corner reveals an architectural gem dating from the thirteenth to the twentieth century, and behind the facades of palaces are interiors of amazing splendour filled with impressive art collections. One of the planet's most walkable cities, you can amble across the centre in an hour through a maze of traffic-free streets; around the edge of the densely built-up historical core are sweeping green spaces where you can sit and enjoy the sunshine and birdsong.

This guide divides Prague into its districts of Hradčany (the Castle District), the Lesser Quarter (Malá Strana), the Old Town (Staré Město) and the New Town (Nové Město). The major historical and architectural attractions of each are highlighted, as well as Prague's illustrious river crossing, the Charles Bridge, linking the city across the Vltava. The city's suburbs also contain several sights worthy of a visit. Finally, there is a selection of day-trips to nearby towns and castles.

HRADČANY (CASTLE DISTRICT)

HIGHLIGHTS

» Hradčany Square, see page 36
» Prague Castle, see page 39
» The Loreto, see page 49
» Strahov Monastery, see page 50

Upon the first glimpse of Prague Castle from across the River Vltava, most visitors are taken aback by its sheer scale. For the erstwhile rulers of Bohemia, a simple stone stronghold was not enough – they demanded a citadel as big as a small town, its cluster of buildings an imposing reminder of the power of royalty through the centuries. From its beginnings some one thousand years ago, the fortress developed to perform important ceremonial functions in addition to its protective ones. In more recent times, part of the castle was revamped to house the office of the president of Czechoslovakia.

The site for the castle was picked because of its ridge-top position, which affords excellent views of the town and river valley below. Today's visitors are faced with a choice of three entrances, of which the ceremonial gate at the west side is the starting point of most guided tours. From here you will be walking downhill towards the steps on the eastern flank.

HRADČANY SQUARE

Before entering the castle take a look around **Hradčany Square** ❶ (Hradčanské náměstí), which forms an irregular open space outside the gates. A smattering of important grand residences was built here in close proximity to the seat of power. In a small grassy area at the centre of the square stands a plague column, one of many erected by grateful survivors after an outbreak of the disease in the eighteenth century.

On the west side of the square are the **Tuscan Palace** (Toskánsky palác), a late seventeenth-century Baroque residence thought to have been designed by French architect Jean-Baptiste Mathey, and the neighbouring **Martinic Palace** (Martinický palác), in earlier Renaissance style. The former now belongs to the foreign ministry, while renovations to the latter revealed *sgraffito* (patterns incised on a flat wall of plaster to create a three-dimensional effect of shade and depth) depicting biblical scenes.

Across the park, **Schwarzenberg Palace** ❷ (Schwarzenberský palác) is the most distinctive building on the square. Each facade is etched with brick-like *sgraffito*, its purpose being to link the disparate architectural styles of the building into a coherent whole. The palace was built for the Lobkowicz family by the Italian

The National Gallery at the Sternberg Palace

architect Agostini Galli in the mid-1500s, which lent it far more of a Florentine influence than other buildings of the time. The palace is now home to the National Gallery's superb collection of **Old Masters** (Hradčanské náměstí 2; www.ngprague.cz; charge), which features works by two of the most important Czech painters of the era, Petr Brandl (1668–1735) and Jan Kupecký (1667–1740). Next to it stands the **Salm Palace** (Salmovský palác) which also belongs to the National Gallery but is only open for temporary exhibitions.

The most ornate building on the square is the **Archbishop's Palace** (Arcibiskupský palác), sitting just next to the castle entrance. The house became the Archbishop's Palace after the Counter-Reformation in 1562 and its position was an indication of the power of the Catholic Church and its influence on the Habsburg monarchy. The facade was redesigned in the 1760s in rococo style.

Next door is another of the major art galleries of Prague. A cobbled alleyway leads to **Sternberg Palace ❸** (Šternberský palác, Hradčanské náměstí 15; www.ngprague.cz; charge), home of Franz Sternberg who was a great patron of the arts during the late eighteenth century. The handsome Baroque building now houses another branch of the National Gallery, its collection picking up where the Schwarzenberg Palace leaves off. The Old Masters displayed here date from the fourteenth to the eighteenth century and serve as a reminder that the Habsburg dynasty was the most powerful of its time, ruling over its vast empire, in which Prague was an important component. Their collection incorporates work by the finest artists of their respective eras. Flemish and Dutch art features particularly strongly with works by the Brueghel dynasty, along with Peter Paul Rubens, Rembrandt and Frans Hals. Italian artists are represented by a wealth of fourteenth- and fifteenth-century decorative pieces from churches in Tuscany. Among the

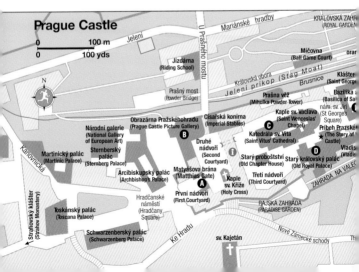

later paintings, standouts include works by Tintoretto and El Greco. Perhaps the most noted painting in the curation is to be found in the Austrian and German section. Along with works by Hans Holbein and his son hangs the *Feast of the Rose Garlands* by Albrecht Dürer, with two Habsburg family members depicted on the canvas.

PRAGUE CASTLE

Building work on **Prague Castle ❹** (Pražský hrad; www.hrad.cz) began in the ninth century. By the beginning of the fourteenth

century, it housed the royal palace, churches and a monastery. Refurbished during the reign of Charles IV, it was ravaged by fire in 1541 and most of the buildings were reconstructed in Renaissance style. The castle eventually became a backwater when the Habsburgs chose Vienna as their permanent base, but in the mid-eighteenth century it was given its present unified appearance by Empress Maria Theresa and her Italian architect Nicola Pacassi. After Czechoslovak independence in 1918, it became the seat of the country's president, with sections

The Golden Portal, once the main entrance to the cathedral

given a rather idiosyncratic makeover by Slovene architect Josep Plečnik. Surrounding the walls are gardens offering a peaceful escape from the often-crowded rooms and galleries within.

Enter the castle proper through the ornate gates crowned with heroic statues of fighting giants. Sombre, uniformed guards maintain a silent watch as you pass through. From this first courtyard – added in the eighteenth century – the **Matthias Gate** Ⓐ (Matyášova brána), the entranceway dating from 1614 that once formed a triumphal arch over moats (now filled in) leads to the second courtyard. Immediately ahead is the entrance to the **Holy Cross Chapel** (kaple svatého Kříže), built by Anselmo Lurago in 1753, which houses a display of the cathedral's numerous national treasures and the remains of some of the country's most revered individuals (free).

Housed on the north side of this courtyard, in what were once the castle stables, is the **Prague Castle Picture Gallery** **B** (Obrazárna Pražského hradu; www.hrad.cz; charge). The gallery displays works mainly collected by Rudolf II during his reign (1583–1612). Much of the collection of this passionate man of the arts was taken to Vienna in the years after his reign or lost to the Swedish forces who took it as booty in 1648.

Still, the gallery boasts some superb works by Tintoretto, Veronese and Rubens. Here, visitors can also enter the north gardens through an archway.

St Vitus Cathedral

A narrow passage leads to the third courtyard of the castle and a sudden view of the immense facade of **St Vitus Cathedral** **C** (katedrála svatého Víta; www.katedralasvatehovita.cz; charge), looming up just a few steps away. The soaring towers and spires dwarf the surrounding buildings, at first glance altering one's perception of architectural scale.

The first church on this hallowed spot was built in the tenth century by Prince Wenceslas, who was interred in the rotunda after his premature death. The present edifice was begun in 1344 when Prague was promoted to an archbishopric. Charles IV decided that the new cathedral should be in the style of the great religious

---

NOTES

Of particular note over the triple-arched arcade of the Golden Portal is the mosaic of the Last Judgement, created by Venetian artists in 1370. It is composed of glass, pieces of quartz and other natural stones, as well as sheets of gold leaf slipped between two stones for a gilded effect. The Virgin Mary, John the Baptist, the Apostles, Charles IV and his wife Elizabeth of Pomerania are all represented, not forgetting the six patron saints of Bohemia.

buildings of France and invited Matthew of Arras to design and build it. After Matthew's death, the work was continued by Peter Parler, a German architect, then by his two sons. Work was disrupted during the Hussite uprisings and was intermittent through the following centuries, in fact the whole building was not regarded as complete until 1929, a symbolic moment for the newly hatched Czechoslovakia.

The main entrance is now through the west doorway, but until the nineteenth century it was the south door – or Golden Portal – that provided access.

The porch of the latter doorway is highly decorated and crowned with an ornate mosaic of the *Last Judgement*. To the left, a Gothic window is filled with gold filigree work.

WHERE TO SHOOT THE BEST PICTURES

Staré Město, Prague's historic heart, radiates medieval charm throughout its intricate web of narrow lanes. Photogenic big-hitters include Staroměstské náměstí, the city's showpiece main square, and Charles Bridge, one of Europe's most impressive medieval structures. Arrive early to beat the crowds. Prague Castle (Pražský hrad) towers above the rest of the city, protected by its palatial facade. Before passing through the early Baroque Matthias Gate (Matyášova brána) into the second courtyard, stop and take a picture of the gate itself. St Vitus Cathedral will make an excellent shot from many points in the third courtyard, but it can be hard to squeeze it all in. The small, interlinking Castle Gardens are among the city's loveliest parks, with wonderful views. For the best frames, try the Jižní zahrady (South Gardens) for fine vistas over the city and the Královská zahrada (Royal Gardens), which provide a better view of the cathedral and the bridges of the Vltava. For a striking contrast to the rest of the vast castle complex in which it stands, head to Zlatá ulička (Golden Lane), a picturesque alley of small pastel-toned cottages built in the sixteenth century for Rudolf II's castle guard.

Once visitors have entered the cathedral, its gigantic proportions are immediately apparent. There are over eighteen separate chapels lining the walls. The nineteenth- and twentieth-century elements of the cathedral (near the main entrance) contain a chapel with **stained glass by Alfons Mucha**, greatly admired for his Art Nouveau artwork. However, the eye is automatically drawn down the core of the building to the magnificent **chancel** built by Parler in the 1370s. The towering vaults, decorated with delicate tracery, are a high point in Gothic architectural achievement. These are underpinned by elaborate stained-glass windows.

Stained-glass window by Alfons Mucha in the cathedral

Several of the chapels in this area of the cathedral deserve further examination but none more so than **Wenceslas Chapel** (kaple svatého Václava), dedicated to Saint Wenceslas (the Good King Wenceslas of the famous Christmas carol). Parler created a wonderful Gothic space to house the tomb of the prince, on the same spot as it had been in the previous Romanesque rotunda. The walls are decorated with precious stones and gold leaf interspersed with several ornate frescoes illustrating scenes from the life of the saint. Above the chapel is a small room containing the coronation jewels, the most valuable objects in the whole country. Seven separate keys are needed to unlock the door to the chamber and the jewels remain out of view except for on rare state occasions. Replicas can often be seen displayed at the castle, at Karlštejn and other places around the Czech Republic.

Next to the Wenceslas Chapel are stairs leading to the **crypt** where you can see the walls of earlier religious structures. This room holds the remains of Charles IV and members of his family, along with the tomb of Rudolf II. Above the crypt, in the main level of the cathedral, several other noteworthy rulers are interred: Ferdinand I lies in a large white marble tomb with his wife, and son Maximilian; and an ornate silver tomb holds the remains of Jan of Nepomuk, who was thrown from Charles Bridge in 1393 and declared a saint in the early days of the Counter-Reformation. To the north of the cathedral, you will find the **Mihulka Powder Tower** (Prašná věž), part of the fifteenth-century defensive walls and later used as a foundry and gunpowder workshop. During the reign of Rupert II rumours abounded that experiments in alchemy were being conducted here. It now contains an exhibition dedicated to the history of castle guards.

The silver tomb of John of Nepomuk

The Old Royal Palace

The third courtyard of the castle opens out to the south flank of the cathedral. Walk past the old chapterhouse where you will find a heroic statue of

Vladislav Hall

St George. On the east side of the courtyard is the entrance to the **Old Royal Palace** (Starý královský palác; www.hrad.cz; charge), home to Bohemian rulers from the eleventh century till the Habsburg takeover.

The somewhat modest facade conceals a fascinating building whose architectural style spans several centuries. The Romanesque early palace forms the foundations of the present structure, built during the last years of Přemyslid rule. Charles IV later enlarged the palace, but it was Vladislav Jagiello in the late 1400s who created the opulent throne chamber. When it was completed in 1502, **Vladislav Hall** (Vladislavský sál) was the largest unsupported secular hall in the world and today its wide expanse and roof supported by ribbed vaults is one of Prague's architectural highlights.

The colourful sixteenth-century cottages of Golden Lane

In the seventeenth century the hall was used as a meeting place, but in earlier times royal tournaments were held there with competitions in equestrianism. The horses were ridden up a wide, gently sloping staircase to the hall, which is now used by groups touring the palace. Serious business went on in the two rooms leading off Vladislav Hall. The **Bohemian Chancellery** (Česká kancelář) was used for Bohemian government meetings, and it was from this room that the two imperial councillors and their clerk were defenestrated in 1618, precipitating the Thirty Years' War. The **Diet Hall** (Stará sněmovna) was the medieval parliament room. It was badly damaged in the fire of 1541 and rebuilt in the style of the time.

The Old Royal Palace also houses the unmissable **Story of Prague Castle** exhibition, which uses castle models, films and genuine historical artefacts in an innovative and interactive manner to tell the long and fascinating history of Prague Castle in a digestible way.

St George's Basilica

From the Royal Palace, walk east to another open square: St George's (náměstí U svatého Jiří). On the corner is the deep-red Baroque facade of **St George's Basilica**  (Bazilika svátého Jiří; charge), founded in the early ninth century and said to be the oldest surviving church in Prague. The interior is austere in true Romanesque style, although it has been extensively restored over the centuries, with the scant remains of original ceiling frescos. The basilica is the resting place of Queen Ludmila, patron saint of Bohemia, and other members of the Přemyslid dynasty.

At the end of the ninth century **St George's Convent** (klášter svatého Jiří) was established next to the basilica. The religious sanctuary was rebuilt many times over the centuries before finally being dissolved in 1782.

The eastern sector of the Castle

From the convent it is only a short walk to the eastern sector of the castle. **Golden Lane**  (Zlatá ulička; charge) nestles against the northern ramparts of the castle, lined with a wonderful

Torture chamber in the Dalibor Tower

NOTES

The Singing Fountain, decorated with flowers, animals, Greek gods and a set of bagpipes, is by the Italian sculptor Francesco Terzio. Restoration work has unfortunately meant that the hollow metal of the basin no longer produces music.

array of old cottages dating from the sixteenth century. They were first occupied by archers conscripted to defend the castle and later by craftspeople, including goldsmiths, to whom the street owes its name. Some said that the lane even hosted alchemists for a while. By the beginning of the twentieth century, it was an enclave for the poor. The writer Franz Kafka lived here for a short time in 1916 with his sister. Today the cottages have been restored and are home to souvenir shops and a couple of private galleries. Just watch your head as you enter, as the lintels are extremely low.

Three attractions fill the route from Golden Lane to the east gate. **Lobkowicz Palace** Ⓖ (Lobkovický palác; www.lobkowicz.cz; charge), built in the aftermath of the 1541 fire, houses many of the star items from the outstanding collections of the noble Lobkowicz family. Among them are paintings by Canaletto and Velázquez as well as *Haymaking* by Pieter Brueghel, the pride of the National Gallery before its restitution to its original owners. There are also original scores by Mozart and Beethoven, as well as a large display of armour. Daily classical music concerts take place here.

Across the street, and reached from Golden Lane, are the **Black Tower** (Černá věž), whose origins reach back to the twelfth century, and **Dalibor Tower** Ⓗ (Daliborka), which was used as a prison and named after its first prisoner, a young knight whose plight was also the inspiration for an opera by Czech composer Bedřich Smetana.

Beyond the Black Tower steps lead down to Malostranská Metro station, while to the right is the entrance to the Gardens on the Ramparts, laid out along the castle's southern ramparts. From here it is possible to descend the cliff-like slope to the Lesser Quarter through Palace Gardens below Prague Castle (www.palacove-zahrady.cz), a series of beautifully restored terraced gardens.

The area of Hradčany, although dominated by the castle, offers other attractions to explore. To the north, beyond the deep Stag Moat stands the **Belvedere** (Belvedér), built in the sixteenth century by Ferdinand I and considered to be the very first Italian Renaissance building north of the Alps. It was used as a summerhouse, and the surrounding **Royal Gardens** must have been a welcome area of relaxation for court members. They would have been greatly amused by the **Singing Fountain**, erected in 1568, whose bronze bowls would resonate when hit by the jets of water.

THE LORETO

The Baroque church of the Loreto

Walking west, away from the castle entrance on Hradčany Square, you will arrive at another open square, Loretánské náměstí. Here you will discover the beautifully ornate Baroque facade of the **Loreto** ❺ (Loreta; www.loreta.cz; charge), one of Bohemia's most important centres of Christian pilgrimage.

Its origins date back to the Counter-Reformation of the 1620s when, in order to increase faith in the Catholic religion, the Habsburgs built replicas of the sacred Santa

Casa of Loreto in Italy all across their empire. It's claimed the original Santa Casa (Holy House and home of the Virgin Mary) had been carried by holy men – or transported by angels – from Nazareth when Islam overran the Holy Land at the turn of the first millennium.

However, Prague's replica **Santa Casa** soon developed into far more than a simple shrine. By 1661 it was surrounded by handsome cloisters, to be followed by Baroque decoration and a distinctive belltower created by Christoph and Kilián Ignác Dientzenhofer (father and son), two of the most skilled architects of their time. Gifts poured in from around the kingdom, and the treasury of the Loreto displays its amazing wealth, including a gold-plated and diamond-encrusted monstrance dating from 1699.

Across the square from the Loreto is the expansive facade of **Černín Palace** (Černínský palác), which occupies the entire western flank. Built for the Černíns, an influential diplomatic family in the seventeenth century, the palace was huge, measuring an astounding 150m (500ft) in length. Its size was even said to have displeased Leopold I who felt that it rivalled the Royal Palace in splendour. Today it houses the Czech Foreign Ministry, and it was from one of these windows that Jan Masaryk (son of the first Czechoslovak president and father of the nation Tomáš Masaryk) mysteriously fell to his death in 1948 as the communists seized power.

A PRICELESS LIBRARY

The Strahov Monastery holds some 130,000 volumes, of which three thousand are manuscripts (the oldest one is the Strahov Gospel) and two thousand first editions. The library also has the distinction of housing the manuscript of the Gerlaci Chronicon (1220) and the first edition of the work by Nicholas Copernicus, De Revolutionibus Orbium Cœlestium ('On the Revolution of the Celestial Orbs'), in which the famous astronomer explains that it is the earth that revolves around the sun and not vice versa.

North of the square lies one of the prettiest, most unspoiled districts in Prague. **Nový Svět** was formerly the poorest quarter in the castle district and as such was left undeveloped.

STRAHOV MONASTERY

Situated a couple of minutes south of Loreto Square and overlooking the river and city is **Strahov Monastery ❻** (Strahovský klášter; www. strahovskyklaster.cz; charge), founded in 1140. The complex was situated outside the protection of the city at

Strahov's Philosophical Library

the end of the road linking Bohemia to what is now Germany, and it was the first such building for the Premonstratensian order. By devoting itself to research it continued to function until 1952 when it was dissolved by the communist regime and the complex taken over for museums. Little remains of the original Romanesque buildings save traces of Gothic and Renaissance features. The monastery is now almost wholly Baroque in style, including two distinctive white towers.

The monastery's greatest treasures are the magnificent **Theological and Philosophical Libraries**, which were built in 1672 and the late 1700s, respectively, and can be viewed from the doorway. The walls are a sight to behold, lined from top to bottom with bookcase upon bookcase of polished timber filled with numerous valuable editions, all aged parchment bound in leather. The eye is drawn up the cases to the highly decorated frescoed ceilings. The eighteenth-century cabinet of curiosities in the connecting hall houses, among other things, a faked chimera and two whale penises. One religious building remains, the **Basilica of the Assumption of the Virgin Mary** (Bazilika Nanebevzetí Panny Marie), with its rococo gilding and ceiling paintings of cherubs. Mozart is said to have played the organ in the church in 1787. Another reason to visit the monastery is to sip the beer produced by the monastery brewery for over six centuries.

MALÁ STRANA

HIGHLIGHTS
» Lesser Quarter Square, see page 52
» Kampa Island and Petřín Hill, see page 56
» Charles Bridge, see page 57

Lying below the castle and stretching to the banks of the Vtlava River is **Malá Strana**, the Lesser Quarter or Little Quarter. The area was first settled in the thirteenth century when Otakar II invited German craftspeople to settle in Prague. Several fierce fires destroyed the early town, so although the street plan remains faithful to Otakar's original instructions, the majority of the buildings date from a later period. Following the Counter-Reformation in the mid-seventeenth century, Malá Strana became fashionable with courtiers and aristocrats, and their money was invested in mansions replete with Renaissance and Baroque details. This is still a residential area, a factor which gives it an intimate atmosphere tangibly different to that of Staré Město just across the river (see page 59).

LESSER QUARTER SQUARE
The heart of this quarter is **Lesser Quarter Square** (Malostranské náměstí), lined by fine palaces (one of which houses the Czech

Parliament) with the arcades that straddle the cobblestones. This is the only part of Malá Strana that ever feels busy with tourists milling around, office workers heading for meetings, and a busy tram stop on the eastern side. Splitting the square in two is the **Church of St Nicholas** ❼ (kostel svatého Mikuláše; www.stnicholas.cz; charge). A prominent building on the Prague skyline and one of the architectural highlights of the city, the church is perhaps the crowning glory of the Dientzenhofer dynasty. Work began in the first years of the eighteenth century but was not finished until 1755. The distinctive 75m (245ft) dome dominates the surrounding buildings. The now-renovated interior of the church is a Baroque masterpiece, with ceiling frescoes by the Viennese artist Johann Lukas Kracker featuring scenes from the life of St Nicholas,

Emblem of the House at the Three Fiddles, on Nerudova

Boat on the canal at Kampa Island

and Franz Palko's *Celebration of the Holy Trinity* gracing the inside of the dome. The two statues below that of St Nicholas above the altar are of St Ignatius Loyola and St Francis Xavier. The church organ has 2500 pipes and 44 registers, and was once played by Mozart. The bell-tower can be climbed for views across the red roofs of Malá Strana. This vantage point was once used by the communist secret police to spy on diplomats from the many embassies in the neighbourhood.

To the north of the square is Letenská Street where you will find the **Church of St Thomas** (kostel svatého Tomáše) abutting the road. Originally founded in 1257, it was one church that remained Catholic throughout the Hussite uprising, and at the onset of the Counter-Revolution became a major focus of Catholic worship. In 1723 the church was badly damaged during a storm, and Kilian Ignaz Dientzenhofer was commissioned to oversee its rebuilding. St Thomas was once the church of a large monastery that had the sole right to brew beer within Prague; the brewery closed in 1951, but the cellar is now home to the atmospheric *Refectory Bar* within the *Augustine Restaurant*.

As you walk towards Malostranská metro station you pass the high walls of **Wallenstein Palace** (Valdštejnský palác; www.senat.cz). Now the home of the Czech Senate (the upper house of the

Czech Parliament), this extensive complex was the first Baroque palace in Prague and was built for Albrecht von Wallenstein, a favourite military commander of Ferdinand II. He began work on the palace in 1624 but soon fell victim to his own publicity: he was killed on the king's orders in 1634 when he was discovered to be holding secret talks with the enemy. The **gardens** (free) feature a superb loggia, clipped hedges, fountains and statuary: copies of works by the celebrated sculptor Adriaen de Vries – the originals having been stolen by Swedish forces during the Thirty Years' War.

West of Lesser Quarter Square is **Nerudova**, named after writer Jan Neruda, who once lived here. There is a string of fine buildings on this street, each distinguished by an emblem as they were built before the introduction of street numbers. Look out for 'The Three Fiddles' at No. 12 or 'The Green Lobster' at No. 43. Thun-Hohenstein Palace at No. 20, its ornate entranceway framed by huge eagles, is now the Italian Embassy; the Morzin Palace at No. 5 serves as a diplomatic base for Romania.

South of Lesser Quarter Square, the houses are a little less grand, but the streets are peaceful and often devoid of tourist shops. Walk down Karmelitská to find the rather plain **Church of Our Lady of Victories** (kostel Panie Marie Vítězná; www.pragjesu.info; free) on your right, named in honour of the victory at the Battle of White Mountain in 1620. Many visitors from southern Europe make a pilgrimage here to see the Holy Infant of Prague (Bambino di Praga) – a wax effigy brought from Spain in 1628 and said to work miracles.

From the church, cross the street and head east to **Maltese Square** (Maltézské náměstí), filled with Baroque palaces, some of which are now embassy buildings. The square is named after the knights of Malta who were granted the nearby twelfth-century **Church of Our Lady Beneath the Chain** (kostel Panny Marie pod řetězem; www.maltezskyrad.cz; sightseeing by appointment only or before the mass) as a gift from King Vladislav. Here they built a large priory that provided protection for the Judith Bridge across

Charles Bridge

the Vltava. The church's odd name refers to the chain used to close the monastery gates. Just round the corner at Saská 3 lies the little-visited **Karel Zeman Museum** (Muzeum Karla Zemana; www.muzeumkarlazemana.cz; charge) where you can explore the fantastical world of this famous Czech film director and animator through interactive exhibits.

KAMPA ISLAND AND PETŘÍN HILL

Located nearby, Grand Priory Square (Velkopřevorské náměstí) leads across a bridge to **Kampa Island** ❽. Here you will find one of Prague's oddest tourist attractions – the **Lennon Wall**. Once adorned with a mural of John Lennon that became a focus for youth unrest in the final days of communist rule, since the 1990s the wall has become a slightly controversial site, whitewashed over several times and permanently daubed with tourist graffiti. It's certainly not the place of protest it once was. Nearby, the narrow branch of the river separating Kampa Island from the Lesser Quarter was once used to power watermills and is rather fancifully dubbed 'Prague Venice'. Most of the island is now parkland, though at its northern end is na Kampě, a delightful cobbled square. A large mill on the banks of the Vltava has been imaginatively converted into the **Museum Kampa** (www.museumkampa.cz; charge), with collections of twentieth-century and contemporary art. Head down Karmelitská and, as it becomes Újezd, you will see **Petřín Hill** ❾. Footpaths wind up to the summit, but it is far less taxing to take the **funicular** (www.dpp.cz). At the top you will find the **Observation Tower** – a mini Eiffel Tower built for the Prague Industrial Exhibition in 1891; a mirror maze; two chapels and a church; and the remnants of the **Hunger Wall** (Hladová zeď) – a city wall built by Charles IV and said to have been a community project to provide work, and therefore food, for the poor. Not far from the Hunger Wall, on Ujezd, is the stark **Monument to the Victims of Communism**, unveiled in 2002.

CHARLES BRIDGE

East of Lesser Quarter Square is Mostecká (Bridge Street), which leads to the river and one of the highlights of any visit to Prague: **Charles Bridge** ❿ (Karlův most). This 520m (1700ft) -long bridge was built across the Vltava in the mid-fourteenth century following the destruction of the previous Judith Bridge in a flood. Charles IV and his architect, Peter Parler, were determined to build a span that would endure, but even they could not have imagined that it would last six hundred years and counting. The original design was a very functional structure with little embellishment. At the Malá Strana end there were two towers: the **Judith Tower** (c.1190), the smaller of the pair, survives as the only reminder of the Judith Bridge. The Lesser Quarter Bridge Tower was built as a gateway to the town. At the Old Town end of the bridge is the **Old Town Bridge Tower**, a masterpiece of Gothic architecture. Both towers are open to the public and offer splendid views of the city.

The numerous statues that now make the bridge unmistakeable were mainly added in the early eighteenth century when the Italian fashion for bridge decoration spread throughout Europe. The exception to this is the sculpture of **St John Nepomuk**, which was erected in 1683 on what was thought to be the 300th anniversary of his violent demise at the hands of King Wenceslas

The relief depicting the demise of St John Nepomuk

IV. When his lifeless body was thrown from the bridge, onlookers claimed that a holy spirit was seen rising from it, and the story heightened his revered status. The bronze relief below Nepomuk's statue, the one with five stars on the halo around the head, depicts the final moment of the saint; it is polished each day by the hands of thousands of tourists who hope it brings good luck.

The bridge carried traffic until the 1950s – until the mid-nineteenth century it was the only way to cross the river – but is now reserved for pedestrians. During the day Charles Bridge can be one of the busiest parts of the city, as the tourist hordes march determinedly between stops on the Royal Way, the erstwhile route the kings of Bohemia took between the Powder Tower and the castle. Artists set up stalls along its path to tempt you with watercolours or moody black-and-white photographs while the odd busker entertains the crowds. The **Charles Bridge Museum** (Museum Karlova Mostu; Křižovnické náměstí 3; www. muzeumkarlovamostu.shop; charge) tells the story of the bridge.

STARÉ MĚSTO (OLD TOWN)

HIGHLIGHTS

While Hradčany was the seat of royal and church power, the **Old Town** (Staré Město) – a cluster of streets on the opposite bank of the river – was the commercial heart of Prague. The city once straddled important trading routes, east–west from Kraków into Germany and north–south from Vienna to Warsaw. As the Bohemian *groschen* became one of the major currencies in Europe, so the city began to take on a grander appearance. Today it offers streets of architectural delights from the medieval to the Baroque. At its heart, the Old Town Square is the obvious place to kick off a tour.

OLD TOWN SQUARE

Often considered Prague's epicentre, the **Old Town Square** ⓫ (Staroměstské náměstí) is a focus for tour groups, bars, cafés and most excesses of the city's tourist industry. Of a large, irregular shape that has changed over the centuries, it has been dominated in modern times by a powerful **Monument to Jan Hus** (pomník Jana Husa), unveiled in 1915 on the 500th anniversary of the martyr's death. This was joined in 2020 by a very tall **Marian Column** (Mariánský sloup), a replica that now stands on the site of the original which was torn down in 1918.

The Astronomical Clock

The **Old Town Hall** ⓬ (Staroměstská radnice; www.prague.eu; charge) sits on the southwest corner of the square. A curious amalgamation of architectural styles – its earliest elements date from the fourteenth century – it expanded as Prague grew in importance. Badly damaged in the final days of World War II, the north wing was never rebuilt.

Although many interesting features adorn the exterior of the building, most visitors crowd to see the **Astronomical Clock** which was added in 1490. At the time, it was so highly prized by the city fathers that they had the clockmaker who made it blinded so that he could not re-create his masterpiece. On the hour, the figures on the clock perform their ritual. Death consults his watch and pulls a cord that rings a bell; Christ and the apostles appear above; and the crowing of a cock signals the end of the proceedings. The clock captures time in a variety of ways, from the passing seconds to the cycles of the sun and moon. It is interesting to note that, in keeping with the thinking of the time, the clock shows the earth positioned at the centre of the universe.

You can visit the inside of the Old Town Hall to see the council chambers with their superb tapestries and the Oriel Chapel. Climb the Old Town Hall Tower, erected in 1364, for an excellent view of the surrounding streets and rooftops. Abutting the Old Town Hall is **Dům U Minuty**. With its distinctive *sgraffito* decoration, it is one of the most memorable Renaissance buildings in Prague.

The west flank of the square altered dramatically in the late twentieth century. A large, open area behind the Old Town Hall was cleared following the devastation wreaked during the last days of the German occupation. It now has benches where weary tourists can take a rest. The ornate facade of the **Church of St Nicholas** (kostel svatého Mikuláše; www.svmikulas.cz) was once hidden down a narrow side street but today it appears as part of the north flank. Although a church has occupied this site since the twelfth century, the present building dates from 1735. During World War I it served as the church of the Prague garrison, and at the end of the conflict was handed over to the constituted Czechoslovak Church. It is often used for classical music concerts.

The east flank is dominated by two buildings. The eye-catching rococo facade belongs to **Kinský Palace** (palác Kinských), designed by Kilian Deintzenhofer and built from 1755–65 by Anselmo Lurago. Kafka's father had a shop in the building and the writer himself attended the German grammar school on the upper floors. In 1948, from the palace balcony, Klement Gottwald made a speech that was instrumental in the communist takeover of the government. The palace is now part of the National Gallery (www.

EXECUTION SQUARE

The Old Town Square used to serve as a backdrop for public gatherings but also executions. In 1437, 56 Hussite soldiers mounted the scaffold. On 21 June 1621, the 27 leaders of the uprising of 1618 were executed on the order of King Ferdinand II. Their number was made up of noblemen and ordinary citizens, Germans and Czechs alike. Twenty-four of the condemned were put to death by the same executioner. The event is commemorated by a plaque set in the wall of the Old Town Hall along with crosses planted in the ground.

Church of Our Lady before Týn

ngprague.cz; charge) and is used for exhibitions.

In stark contrast is the **Church of Our Lady before Týn** ⑬ (kostel Panny Marie před Týnem; www.tyn.cz), an immense Gothic edifice whose fifteenth-century towers rise to eighty metres (260ft) above the surrounding medieval streets. The church was a hotbed of heresy from its earliest days and became the main Hussite place of worship as the reform movement grew in popularity during the sixteenth century. Following the Counter-Reformation, it was handed back to the Catholic Church and has remained steadfast to the present day.

AROUND THE OLD TOWN SQUARE

The streets surrounding the Old Town Square are a delight to explore. Almost every building throws up some highlight, ranging from the tiniest detail – a doorknocker or carved lintel – to the grand statement, for example the superb Renaissance door of the **House at the Two Golden Bears** (Dům u Dvou Zlatých Medvědů), on Melantrichova. There's no better way to explore this part of town than on foot, and much of the Old Town is pedestrianised.

West of Old Town Square, the area extending to the river is probably the most densely packed with fine mansions. However, it also has one of the highest concentrations of tourist shops. Next to

Old Town Square is the much smaller **Malé náměstí**, decorated with a filigree fountain. On the west side of the square, it is the facade of Rott House (U Rotta; www.hotelrott.cz) that steals the show. It's decorated with paintings by acclaimed nineteenth-century Czech artist Mikoláš Aleš.

Karlova or Charles Street is the most direct route to Charles Bridge. Look out for the **Clam-Gallas Palace** (Clam-Gallasův palác), a magnificent Baroque building set with gargantuan statues by Matthias Bernard Braun. Just before you reach the river you will pass the high walls of the **Clementinum** ⓮ (Klementinum; www.klementinum.com; charge), a former Jesuit college and the largest complex of buildings on this side of the river. The site was originally the Dominican monastery of St Clement, but was offered to the Jesuit brotherhood by Ferdinand I in 1556 to promote Catholic education. Work commenced on the Church of the Holy Saviour in 1593, and its domes now describe one of the most recognisable outlines in the city. By the middle of the seventeenth century the Jesuits had a monopoly on education in the city as the Hussite faculty of the Carolinum (see page 71) was disbanded.

The Clementinum expanded as the university grew, resulting in a large part of the Old Town being demolished in 1653, although this process was not completed until one hundred years later. When the Jesuit brotherhood was dissolved by papal decree in 1773, the Clementinum became home to the library of the secular Charles University. Today it is the **National Library**, and its churches are used as venues for concerts. Also on the site is the fascinating Astronomical Tower, offering fine views over the Old Town.

The approach to Charles Bridge is marked by the small Knights of the Cross Square (Křižovnické náměstí), watched over by a majestic statue of Charles IV erected here in 1848 to mark the 500th anniversary of the founding of Charles University. On the north side is the **Church of the Knights of the Cross** dedicated to St Francis Seraphicus (svatého Františka Serafinského). The

French-style Pařížská

one church is only open for services. South of the bridge is the Novotného lávka, a jetty lined with buildings. Furthest away, with a wonderful view of the river, bridge and castle is the **Smetana Museum** (Muzeum Bedřicha Smetany; www.nm.cz; charge), which pays homage to one of the country's most beloved composers and musicians.

South of Karlova is Bethlehem Square (Betlémské náměstí) where you will find a reproduction of the fourteenth-century **Bethlehem Chapel** (Betlémská kaple; www.bethlehemchapel.eu; charge). It was here that Jan Hus embarked on his campaign to reform the Catholic Church, which ended in his execution. One main form of protest consisted in conducting Mass in Czech instead of Latin. Just around the corner from here is the **Rotunda of the Holy Cross**, one of the three remaining Romanesque round churches in Prague.

THE JEWISH QUARTER

North of Old Town Square is **Josefov**, once the base of one of the most active and influential Jewish communities in Eastern Europe and still home to a small Orthodox community. To reach Josefov, walk down **Pařížská** ⑮, by the side of the Church of St Nicholas. This street, as the name suggests, is reminiscent of a leafy Paris boulevard complete with fine boutiques.

The Jewish community was founded in the latter years of the eleventh century. Throughout the centuries the Jews were alternatively accepted and ostracised by the ruling dynasties. Certainly, they were never allowed to expand beyond this small quarter. Despite a devastating fire in 1689 and the demolition of many buildings in the quarter in the 1890s to make way for new, more sanitary, housing, several important buildings remain. In the days leading to the genocide of the Jews by the Nazis in World War II, the treasures of numerous synagogues in Bohemia were brought to Prague for safekeeping and in order that a museum might be founded to document an extinct race. The collection is managed by the **Jewish Museum** (www.jewishmuseum.cz; charge), which oversees several museums housed in the Josefov synagogues.

The **Old-New Synagogue** 🔟 (Staronová synagóga; not part of the Jewish Museum; www.synagogue.cz; charge) is the oldest surviving synagogue in Europe. Built at the beginning of the thirteenth century, it was named the New Synagogue but renamed Old-New when a newer synagogue, now demolished, was built

THE GOLEM

The giant man of clay called the Golem is Prague's equivalent of the Frankenstein monster. He is supposed to have been fashioned out of mud from the riverside by learned Rabbi Loew (c.1520–1609), master of many an arcane mystery. Obedient at first, the Golem performs his allotted tasks, but runs amok when the rabbi forgets to renew the charm that keeps him under control. Eventually he is overcome, and a spell reduces him once more to mud. His remains are shovelled up and stored among the rafters in the attic of the Old-New Synagogue, where they have been ever since. Woe betide anyone who has the temerity to disturb them! The most enduring image of the Golem is the one in the film of the same name, a silent-screen classic of the early cinema by the German director Paul Wegener.

nearby. It is one of the finest medieval buildings in the city. The main hall is reached through a small, arched doorway featuring an elaborate carving of a vine; the twelve bunches of grapes depict the twelve tribes of Israel. The interior walls bear traces of thirteenth-century frescoes and later inscriptions of sections of the Psalms. The brick sawtooth gables on the exterior were added in the fifteenth century. Next to the synagogue is the **Jewish Town Hall** (Židovská radnice), the seat of the Chief Rabbi. Its pink, Baroque facade is crowned by a fine tower and two clocks, which tell the time in Hebrew and Roman numerals.

The entrance to a complex of two synagogues and the Jewish Cemetery lies on Široká. The ticket office here offers a special rate for one or all of the Jewish Museum attractions; alternatively, you can buy tickets at each separate venue. At this site, the **Pinkas Synagogue** (Pinkasova synagóga; www.jewishmuseum.cz) began life as a private family place of worship, although it was later expanded to rival the Old-New Synagogue. Following the end of World War II, the names of all the Czech victims of the Holocaust were inscribed on the walls of this synagogue in a stark and powerful tribute to those who lost their lives.

Make your way through the outer courtyard of the Synagogue to reach the **Old Jewish Cemetery** (Starý židovský hřbitov; www.jewishmuseum.cz; charge). This small area was once the only burial ground for Jews and as such, each plot was used by several generations of the same family. It is thought that over 12,000 gravestones were placed here, the earliest surviving ones dating from 1429 and the most recent from 1787. The jumble of carved stones sits beneath the shade of mature trees. The **Ceremonial Hall** next to the cemetery was built in 1911 for the Prague Burial Society and now has an exhibition on Jewish life and traditions.

The **Klausen Synagogue** (Klausová synagóga) resides on the far side of the cemetery and was built on the ruins of a school, or *klausen*, in 1694. It displays artefacts relating to Jewish history and customs, including biographical information about the major figures of the Jewish community of Prague such as Rabbi Löw, who was suspected of working with the supernatural. His ornate tomb in the cemetery is regularly visited by well-wishers who have come to pay their respects. The Jewish Museum is responsible for two other synagogues. Nearby, **Maisel Synagogue** (Maiselova synagóga), on Maiselova, also began life as a private house of prayer belonging to Mordachai Maisel who acted as banker to Emperor Rudolf II. The original structure was lost in the fire of 1689, but replaced by this ornate building, and it makes a fine backdrop to the collection of treasures it displays. Rare items of religious significance dating back to the Renaissance, including liturgical silver, textiles and manuscripts, can be viewed here.

The Old Jewish Cemetery

The Spanish Synagogue

Finally, a comparatively recent addition to the Jewish Museum is perhaps its crowning jewel. The **Spanish Synagogue** ⑰ (Španělská synagóga; www.jewishmuseum.cz), a little way east on Vězeňská, has been renovated and its 1860s Moorish architectural style and wall decoration are truly dazzling. The richness of the interior is in total contrast with the simplicity of the Old-New Synagogue. Displays recount the recent history of the Czech Jewish community.

ON THE BANKS OF THE VLTAVA

On the outskirts of the Josefov are three attractions that are in no way associated with the Jewish community. The beautifully laid-out **Museum of Decorative Arts** (Umělecko-průmyslové muzeum; www.upm.cz; charge) occupies a French-style Neoclassical building whose rear overlooks the Old Jewish Cemetery. It is a showcase for all types of decorative art, at which the inhabitants of Bohemia have consistently excelled. The museum holds one of the world's largest collections of antique glass. There are also displays relating to ceramics, tapestries, costumes and clocks.

In the direction of the river stands the impressive, neo-Renaissance facade of the **Rudolfinum** (www.rudolfinum.cz), one of the finest concert venues in the city and home to the Czech Philharmonic Orchestra. It served as the seat of the Czechoslovak parliament immediately after independence in 1918.

Also on the banks of the Vltava, but a little way north, is **St Agnes' Convent** ⑱ (klášter svaté Anežsky). The convent was founded in the first half of the thirteenth century by the Poor Clares, and at its prime was a large complex of several churches and cloisters before falling into decay. Today the remaining buildings have been restored to house the National Gallery's outstanding collection of **Medieval Art in Bohemia and Central Europe: 1200–1550** (www.ngprague.cz; charge), including works by Master Theodoric, Lucas Cranach the Elder and Albrecht Dürer. The convent also acts as a venue for concerts and temporary exhibitions.

EAST OF OLD TOWN SQUARE

Beyond the Church of Our Lady before Týn, you will find a collection of narrow lanes sheltering the pretty **Church of St James** (kostel svatého Jakuba), and a wide thoroughfare, **Celetná**. Now free of traffic, it was once the major entry route to the city from the east. A stroll along Celetná reveals fine houses, little alleyways, courtyards and deep cellars. Faint traces of Renaissance Prague are discernible among the Baroque decoration. The **House of the Black Madonna** ⑲ (dům U černé Matky boží) at No. 34 dates from the early twentieth century. The huge windows of this Cubist masterpiece, built by Josef Gočár in 1911–12, reveal its original use as a department store. The statue after which the house is named is located in a niche set on the corner of the facade. Renovated in 1994, the building was home to the National Gallery's Museum of Czech Cubism until 2012, when part of the collection was moved to Veletržní Palace (see page 82). However, the building still houses a Cubist café and shop.

At the eastern end of the street is the **Powder Tower** ⓴ (Prašná brána; www.prague.eu; charge), a tower dating from the end of the thirteenth century. It was one of the gates into the Old Town and marked a transition from the previously favoured defensive structure to a ceremonial entranceway. Originally, it was linked to a palace, called the Royal Court, which was demolished at the beginning of the twentieth century after lying derelict for decades. In its place – in the manner of a phoenix rising from its ashes – is one of Prague's foremost Art Nouveau buildings, the **Municipal House** (Obecní dům; www.obecnidum.cz; tours available, charge). The complex was built in the first decade of the twentieth century with a long list of artists, including Alfons Mucha himself, contributing to the highly decorative interiors and exterior. The idea behind the complex was to provide an exhibition space with a modern auditorium at the heart of the building. The **Smetana Hall** is well established as one of the major arts venues in the city, and has a

House of the Black Madonna

THE ROYAL ROUTE

The Powder Tower marked the start of the so-called Royal Route, the route which the coronation processions of the Bohemian kings and queens took through the city, and which linked Royal Court Palace and the Castle across the river.

Carriages would travel down Celetná, through Old Town Square and along Karlova, before heading across Charles Bridge. Once in Malá Strana they would travel along Mostecká into Lesser Quarter Square before making their way via Nerudova to St Vitus Cathedral in the castle compound. There, the new monarch would be crowned.

sumptuous café, a glittering French restaurant, and a huge, tiled Pilsner beer cellar.

From the Powder Tower, return to the Old Town where one street south of Celetná is Železná, also pedestrianised. Halfway down the street you will see the wrought-iron adornment of the **Estates Theatre** (Stavovské divadlo; www.narodni-divadlo.cz) ahead. Built in the 1780s as the German Theatre, in its lines are some of the finest examples of Neoclassical architecture in the city. Here on 29 October 1878, Mozart conducted the premiere of his new opera *Don Giovanni* in front of a rapturous audience. The theatre was also used as a set for the film *Amadeus*, directed by Czech Miloš Forman.

Next to the theatre lie the remains of the first university of Prague. The **Carolinum** (Karolinum) was founded by Charles IV and named after him. Jan Hus held the post of rector here and the campus became a hotbed of Hussite activity. After the victory of the Counter-Reformation it was handed over to the Catholic Jesuits and merged with their Clementinum complex near the river. Much of what remains here dates from the eighteenth century, but look for the beautiful oriel window overhanging the street between the Carolinum and Estates Theatre.

NOVÉ MĚSTO (THE NEW TOWN)

HIGHLIGHTS

- » Wenceslas Square, see page 72
- » The National Theatre, see page 74
- » Fred and Ginger Building, see page 77

Charles IV gave the go-ahead for the building of the New Town (Nové Město) in 1348 when overcrowding in the Old Town was becoming a problem. Although much has been overshadowed by subsequent redevelopment, the New Town has many key historical attractions. It is also a focus for hotels, museums and stylish shopping in its early twentieth-century covered precincts.

Na příkopě is the street that traditionally divided the Old Town and the New Town. It was built over the old moat, the defensive structure around the Old Town and links to the Powder Gate at its eastern end. Today it is pedestrianised, and is one of Prague's most exclusive retail enclaves, lined with expensive shops, restaurants and casinos.

WENCESLAS SQUARE

The southern end of Na příkopě meets **Wenceslas Square** ㉑ (Václavské náměstí), the symbolic heart of modern Prague for both independent Czechoslovakia and the Czech Republic. The scale of the square is impressive: more of a boulevard than a plaza, at first glance it brings to mind the Champs-Elysées. Huge crowds have gathered here, most notably in 1968 to protest against the arrival of Russian troops, and in 1989 to cheer the fall of communism. Largely closed to traffic, the square is a popular place for a stroll. Pride of place still goes to the **Hotel Evropa**, an Art Nouveau gem. It reopened in 2024 after decades of renovation work. Also look out for the Wiehl House with its neo-Renaissance decoration by Mikoláš Aleš on the corner of Vodičkova.

At the top of the square sits the **St Wenceslas Monument**, a statue of the saint astride a noble steed. Locals often meet "pod ocasem" – "below the tail". Beneath the Czechs' most revered patron saint are life-size statues of the others – Ludmila, Vojtěch and Prokop. Czech sculptor Josef Myslbek was the man behind the work which was erected here in 1912.

Behind the monument is the **National Museum** ㉒ (Národní muzeum; www.nm.cz; charge). Created at a time of rising national consciousness in the late 1880s, its neo-Renaissance styling makes a confident statement with a beautifully decorated exterior and grand interior. The building reopened in 2018 after several years of renovations. Inside you'll find collections relating to minerology, archaeology and anthropology, though it's the world-class temporary exhibitions most come here to see.

North of the museum along busy Wilsonova is the Neoclassical **State Opera** (Státní opera; www.narodni-divadlo.cz). Beyond is the **main railway station**, an Art Nouveau gem which seems to be under permanent renovation. Nearby on Panská 7 is the small **Mucha Museum** (www.mucha.cz; charge), dedicated to the Art Nouveau works of Alfons Mucha (1860–1939). Further north, is the excellent **Museum of Communism** (V Celnici 1031/4; www.muzeumkomunismu.cz),

St Wenceslas Monument

Fresco in the Church of Our Lady of the Snows

which offers a fascinating and at times disturbing insight into life under Soviet rule. The bulk of the New Town lies to the southwest of Wenceslas Square, between busy Sokolská Street and the river. Starting at the northwest end of Wenceslas Square and heading towards the Vltava you will come to **Jungmannova**, a prime shopping area.

On the east side of Jungmann Square (Jungmannovo náměstí) is the **Church of Our Lady of the Snows** ㉓ (kostel Panny Marie Sněžné; www.pms.ofm.cz); look out for a curious **Cubist lamppost** outside the northwest entrance. Founded by Charles IV to mark his coronation in 1347, this great Gothic church was intended to have three aisles, but work was interrupted by the Hussite uprising. What remains is the chancel of the original plan, standing on its own and consequently looking completely out of scale in relation to its floor area.

THE NATIONAL THEATRE AND AROUND

Follow Národní in the direction of the river to find the **National Theatre** ㉔ (Národní divadlo; www.narodni-divadlo.cz) and the New National Theatre. The former, an impressive building that adds grace to the riverfront vista, was built in the middle of the nineteenth century as the result of a passionate demand for an independent Czech theatre. In 1881, just before the theatre was due to open, it was razed to the ground by an accidental fire. However, such was the level of national pride at the time that within weeks the money had been raised to rebuild it, and it reopened in 1883 with a performance of Smetana's *Libuše*.

Many of the finest Czech artists of their day were commissioned to work on the theatre, which was renovated in the 1980s when Karel Prager was commissioned to design the New National Theatre so as to expand the complex. This is one of the most striking examples of communist-era architecture in the city, presenting three boxy buildings adorned with facades of glass brick, and acts as a permanent home to the National Theatre Company and Lanterna Magika.

The National Theatre

ARCHITECTURE OLD AND NEW

Next to the river you will see the **Slovanský ostrov** island to your left. The island did not exist until the early eighteenth century, but, following work to shore up its banks, it became the centre of social life in the city. Here, an ancient water tower is linked to the Manés Gallery, an edifice in the Bauhaus style that is one of the best examples of functionalism in Prague. The HQ of the Manés group of artists who take their name from the nineteenth-century artistic dynasty, it has a changing programme of exhibitions.

Further south along Masarykovo nábřeží (Masaryk riverside boulevard), on the corner of Resslova, is another example of modern architecture. The **Tančící dům** (www.tancici-dum.cz), or dancing building, by the architect Frank Gehry, has become known

The 'dancing' towers of the Fred and Ginger Building

MEMORIES OF THE RESISTANCE

On 18 June 1942, the Church of St Cyril and St Methodius became the scene of an unequal battle between the assassins of Reinhard Heydrich, the Nazi governor of Bohemia and Moravia, and German troops. The Czechoslovak parachutists sent from Britain to carry out the assassination threw a bomb at Heydrich's open-top car, then later sought refuge in the crypt. Unfortunately, they had been betrayed. The whole area was sealed off and the crypt attacked by a battalion of the SS. The seven parachutists fought back determinedly for several hours, but their fate was sealed when the fire brigade was brought in to flood their hiding place. Not a single one of them was taken prisoner – they either perished in the fighting or took their own lives rather than surrender.

locally as the Fred and Ginger Building. A glass-and-concrete tower (Ginger) gives the impression of being held by the upright tower (Fred), as if caught in action on the dance floor.

Walk up Resslova to find the **Church of St Cyril and St Methodius** ㉕ (kostel svatého Cyrila a Metoděje). Methodius, regarded as the father of Czech Christianity, was ably accompanied by St Cyril in his mission to preach the gospel. Built in the Baroque period (c.1730), this church was originally dedicated to St Charles Borromeo and served retired priests. It closed in 1783 but in the 1930s was reopened under the auspices of the Czechoslovak Orthodox Church, hence the change of name. The church became embroiled in one of the tragic episodes of World War II when, after they had assassinated the brutal Nazi governor Reinhard Heydrich, his killers were given sanctuary in the crypt.

The Nazis exacted horrific revenge by ordering the village of Lidice to be burnt to the ground, the men shot, and the women and some of the children deported to concentration camps. A small memorial can be found outside the church where bullet

The New Town Hall

holes from the incident are still visible. The crypt has been turned into a memorial museum (www.vhu.cz; charge) with photographs, documents and memorabilia of the event.

The east end of Resslova meets **Charles Square** (Karlovo náměstí), the largest in the city. Laid out in the original city plan of 1348, it used to be the biggest market in Prague known as the Cattle Market. In the mid-nineteenth century the square was grassed over to create parkland, which is now a rather scruffy green patch. The whole thing is slated for rejuvenation in coming years The surrounding office blocks are not particularly exciting but the **Faust House** ㉖ (Faustův dům) has been preserved and refurbished. The history of the house, which was given its Baroque coat in the eighteenth century, stretches back to the fourteenth century, when it belonged to Prince Václav of Opava, an alchemist and natural historian. In the sixteenth century, it was home to Englishman Edward Kelley, charged by Emperor Rudolf II with turning base metal into gold (alchemy was rarely practiced at noble residences themselves due to the fire risk). The many secretive practices carried out here fostered its association with the Faust legend.

Walking north towards the Old Town you will find the **New Town Hall** ㉗ (Novoměstská radnice; www.nrpraha.cz, charge) at the end of Charles Square. Building work started in 1348, and in 1419 it was the site of the First Defenestration of Prague (see page 25). Several additions were made in the sixteenth and eighteenth centuries, but it is the fifteenth-century tower that is the main attraction here – climb it (no lift) for views across the square and beyond. Before leaving the area, take a detour to **U Fleků** on Křemencová (www.ufleku.cz). Now a bit of a minor tourist trap, this beer hall has been open since 1499. It only serves the strong dark beer brewed on its premises.

Close to the I.P. Pavlova metro is the Baroque **Vila Amerika**, completed in 1720. Designed by Kilián Ignáz Dienzenhofer, it was originally used by the Michna family as a summer palace. Today it houses the **Dvořák Museum** ㉘ (Muzeum Antonína Dvořáka; www.nm.cz; charge), with memorabilia relating to one of the greatest Czech composers. There are very worthwhile recitals during the summer, although recorded compositions by Dvořák are played when the musicians are not present. Around the corner, at No. 12–14 Na bojišti, is the **Chalice Restaurant** (U Kalicha; www.ukalicha.cz), the favourite drinking hall of Jaroslav Hašek, author of *The Good Soldier Svejk* and still one of Prague's more authentic, less tourist-plagued pubs.

NOTES

Dvořák composed an impressive number of works in his lifetime: 31 pieces of chamber music, fifty orchestra scores and nine symphonies, including the famous Slavonic Dances.

OUTLYING AREAS

HIGHLIGHTS

» Vyšehrad, see page 80
» National Technical Museum, see page 82
» Trade Fair Palace, see page 82
» Stromovka Park, see page 83
» Mozart Museum, see page 83
» Letná Park, see page 84
» Troja Palace, see page 84
» Vinohrady, see page 85

Many of Prague's suburbs are chock-a-block with dour modern apartment blocks dating from the communism era when the city saw huge growth. However, not all areas outside the historical centre are grim and there are a number of attractions that make a trip out on the metro or tram well worth the effort.

VYŠEHRAD

Vyšehrad (Vyšehrad metro station; www.praha-vysehrad.cz), meaning high castle, has an important place in the Czech national psyche. On this rocky promontory high above the River Vltava, the legendary Přemyslid Princess Libuše foretold the founding of a great city on the banks of the river. She is said to have married a common man and gave birth to the children who would become the founders of the Czech nation. Unfortunately for the swirling legends, archaeological activity can only date the settlement here as far back as the tenth century, making it actually more recent than Prague Castle.

The castle was built around 1085 by the Přemyslid leader Vratislav II and his two successors, who sought to consolidate power within their growing kingdoms. An abbey was also built and, later, a Romanesque basilica. Power was transferred to

Prague Castle by the end of the twelfth century. However, Charles IV breathed new life into Vyšehrad by building fortifications and large mansions in homage to his mother, who was descended from the Přemyslid dynasty. During the Hussite uprising many of the forts were destroyed, to be rebuilt in the late seventeenth century.

From the metro station, a short walk will lead through two gateways and on to a simple stone church. This is **St Martin's Rotunda** (rotunda svatého Martina), one of the oldest churches in Bohemia. Built in the eleventh century, it was restored in the late 1800s. Make your way to the neo-Gothic **Basilica of Saints Peter and Paul** ㉙ (bazilika svatého Petra a Pavla; charge), which was erected on the site of earlier places of worship.

At this time, Vyšehrad's mythical status as the birthplace of the Czech nation was once more gaining favour thanks to a blossoming spirit of nationalism. It was decided that the cemetery here would become a **national cemetery** (www.slavin.cz) for illustrious Czechs, a symbol of national pride.

The graveyard is dotted with fine sculptures carved by the top artists of the times. Composers Antonín Dvořák and Bedřich Smetana, along with the poet Jan Neruda, are among the many Czech cultural giants who rest here.

The eleventh-century St Martin's Rotunda

NATIONAL TECHNICAL MUSEUM

The **National Technical Museum**  (Národní Technické Muzeum; www.ntm.cz; charge) shelters a wealth of machinery relating to humankind's technical achievements. There are sections on astronomy, cinematography, industry and mining. However, the main focus of the museum resides in its array of cars, trains and aeroplanes dating from the days when motorised transport was still in its infancy.

FIRST REPUBLIC ART

Founded in 1995 in the **Trade Fair Palace** (Veletržní palác; www.ngprague.cz; charge), a masterpiece of 1920s architecture, the National Gallery's collection of **First Republic Art** showcases work from the early twentieth century. The redesigned interior

The National Gallery, Trade Fair Palace

of the palace offers a contemporary gallery space very suited to its collection. The exhibition was installed as recently as 2018 when the Czech Republic celebrated one hundred years since the creation of Czechoslovakia in 1918 following World War II. The idea was to bring together in one location all the groundbreaking art that made the 1920s and 1930s a unique time in Central Europe. The most striking collection for many will be the Czech Cubism section with works by Josef Čapek (brother of the author Karel Čapek), Václav Špála and many others. The exhibition also includes oils by Gauguin, Rousseau, Picasso and Van Gogh which were purchased by the newly minted state at the time.

One controversial work you now won't find here is Mucha's *Slav Epic*, a series of giant oils depicting scenes from Slav history. After a few years of being exhibited at the gallery, the massive canvasses were returned to Moravský Krumlov Chateau in South Moravia. Many would like to see them given a permanent home in Prague.

THE EXHIBITION GROUND AND STROMOVKA PARK

The **Stromovka** was for many centuries a royal hunting ground before being designated a public park in 1804. Today its woodland and lakes provide a pleasantly verdant alternative to the sometimes hot and dusty city streets. The **Exhibition Ground** (Výstaviště) was chosen as the location for the Jubilee of 1891, and its large buildings have been used to host regular exhibitions and concerts. Beside the exhibition halls is the **Lapidarium** (www. nm.cz; charge), the National Museum's collection of sculpture. Here you will find some exceptional works, including original statues from Charles Bridge (most on the bridge today are copies).

MOZART MUSEUM

The **Bertramka Villa** ㉜ (www.bertramka.eu; charge) was where Mozart stayed on numerous occasions during his visits to Prague. It is perched on a wooded expanse of land, which in his time would have been quite removed from the hubbub of the city. In 1787 during one of his visits, Mozart composed elements of the opera *Don Giovanni* only hours before the work's debut at the Estates Theatre. The small museum here displays letters and scores in the hand of the great man, along with musical instruments. In summer there are recitals in the courtyard.

LETNÁ PARK

Draped across the banks of the Vltava opposite the Jewish Quarter, **Letná Park** (Letenské sady) is another open space within easy reach of the city centre. It offers superb views upriver and across the Old Town. Visitors are also drawn to a strange modern sculpture that

Prague Public Transport Museum

sits on a concrete plinth overlooking the Vltava. The constantly swaying arm of a giant metronome was installed here after the Velvet Revolution. The spot was once home to the world's largest Stalin statue, which was dynamited in 1962.

TROJA PALACE

Situated to the north of the city on the banks on the Vltava is the huge **Troja Palace** ⓭ (Trojský zámek; www.ghmp.cz; charge; Holešovice metro station then bus 112). Constructed by the architect Jean-Baptiste Mathey as a summer home for the Sternberg family from 1679–85, the palace became the fashionable place in which to be seen. Designed in the classic Italianate style, it has stunning frescoes adorning its interior, the ones in the Grand Hall being particularly impressive. Among the figures depicted are Habsburg emperors Rudolf I and Leopold I. The gardens sloping down to the river were designed in the French style, an innovation in Prague. The palace houses the collection of the **City Gallery**, mainly comprising nineteenth-century Czech painters. Above the palace, on the hill that overlooks the river, are the lovely **Prague Botanical Gardens** (www.botanicka.cz;charge). The most impressive attraction is the Fata Morgana glasshouse, filled with a wide variety of flora from different climatic zones.

BUBENEČ AND STŘEŠOVICE

Just behind the district of Hradčany are Bubeneč and Střešovice. The former comprises large villas and fin-de-siècle apartment blocks, home to diplomats, embassy staff and high-ranking civil servants. Střešovice is similarly bourgeois and home to the worthwhile **Prague Public Transport Museum** (www.dpp.cz; charge), with an interesting array of old trams and buses. Just around the corner is the **Müller Villa** (www.muzeumprahy.cz; charge), the only example of the work of Brno-born Modernist architect Adolf Loos in Prague and built in the late 1920s in his inimitable functionalist style. Further out, in the district of Břevnov, is a park called Obora hvězda. At the centre of the park is the unusual, six-pointed Renaissance palace known as the **Letohrádek hvězda** (www.pamatniknarodnihopisemnictvi.cz; charge) that has on display a huge model of the Battle of Bílá Hora that took place nearby.

VINOHRADY AND ŽIŽKOV

Take metro line A to Jiřího z Poděbrad station, and you will emerge in the fashionable, densely built-up quarter of **Vinohrady**, a largely gentrified neighbourhood though still one full of atmosphere and historical charm. Near the metro station is Prague's most unusual place of worship, the Modernist **Church of the Sacred Heart**, built in 1932 by Slovene architect Josip Plečnik, which has a distinctive, tombstone-shaped clocktower. Behind the church, turn left on Milešovská Street to be confronted by the gargantuan **Television Tower** (www.towerpark.cz; charge). Construction began in the communist era and was completed in 1992. For the best panoramas of the city you can ascend 93 metres (305ft) of the 216m (709ft) edifice to the observation deck.

The building also contains the world's smallest hotel – a one-room affair with amazing views. The tower is actually in the neighbouring district of Žižkov, known for its erstwhile working-class credentials – at one time it was a hotbed of sedition – and large number of local pubs. The hill that rises to the north of the district is home to the **National Monument** ㉞, a large block of granite that houses the Tomb of the Unknown Soldier. On the way up the hill you pass the **Army Museum** (www.vhu.cz; free), with interesting displays on the role of the Czech army during the two world wars.

EXCURSIONS

HIGHLIGHTS

The medieval Karlštejn Castle

The region around Prague is easily reachable by public transport, making the following trips as easy as boarding a bus or train.

KARLŠTEJN

Rising high above the treetops of the winding valley of the River Berounka like a medieval vision come true, **Karlštejn Castle** 🅰 (www.hrad-karlstejn.cz; charge) is one of the country's greatest attractions, drawing crowds of visitors. It was begun by Emperor Charles IV in 1348 as a spiritual retreat and repository for the crown jewels and the sacred relics he collected. The castle's present appearance is partly the result of an over-zealous neo-Gothic rebuild in the nineteenth century.

There are two tours, but unless you arrange Tour II months in advance, you'll be taking Tour I which loops around the imperial palace. Tour II reveals the castle's sacred heart, a sequence of gorgeously decorated interiors. These include the Chapel of St Catherine, with wall paintings set in a matrix of semi-precious stones, and the Chapel of the Holy Cross, with a starry vault and a stunning series of portraits by court painter Master Theodoric. Numbers are limited to sixteen on this tour and it doesn't run in bad weather. Needless to say, it's hopelessly oversubscribed. Away from the castle, hiking trails radiate out in all directions, a great way to escape the tourist crowds.

KŘIVOKLÁT

While Karlštejn is a short train ride from Prague, the medieval castle at **Křivoklát** ㊴ (www.krivoklat.cz; charge) lies deeper in the countryside, high above the River Berounka near the pretty district town of Rakovník, and thus offers a less crowded, more authentically medieval experience. Surrounded by vast forests, it originated as a royal hunting lodge in the twelfth century. Rebuilt and extended, it continued its role as a royal residence and is everything a feudal fortress should be, with sturdy walls and towers frowning down from a commanding height, shielding authentic medieval interiors within. Entry is by guided tour only.

LIDICE

Following the assassination of Reichsprotektor Heydrich on 27 May 1942, the wrath of the Nazis was turned on an unassuming mining village near the steel town of Kladno. On the night of 9 June, **Lidice** ㊲ was sealed off, its menfolk shot and its women and children sent to concentration camps, from which few returned. The village was bulldozed, and its name erased from the record. After the war, a new Lidice was built a short distance away and the site of the original village became a memorial, with a rose garden of remembrance and a **museum** (www.lidice-memorial.cz; free) telling the tragic story in bitter detail.

The Memorial to the Children Victims of the War, Lidice

NELAHOZEVES

On the banks of the Vltava north of Prague, the otherwise ordinary village of **Nelahozeves** ③⑧ has not one, but two attractions, albeit of very different kinds. Music-lovers make their way to the **Dvořák Birthplace Museum** (Památník Antonína Dvořáka; www. antonindvorak.cz; charge), the modest village house where the great composer was born, while rather more visitors head for the **zámek** (www.lobkowicz.cz/nelahozeves; charge). After the fall of communism, this splendid Renaissance castle was returned to its original owners, the princely Lobkowicz family, who completed its restoration. Begun in the mid-sixteenth century, the castle is extravagantly *sgraffitoed* on the outside and has a succession of opulent interiors reflecting the high status of what was one of the kingdom's leading families.

MĚLNÍK

Visible from far away across the plain, the castle and church of the little town of **Mělník**  crown the bluff high above the confluence of the Vltava with the Elbe (Labe). With its origins in the ninth century, the castle was the place where the future 'Good King' Wenceslas (born around 907) was tutored in the ways of Christianity by his grandmother, Princess Ludmila. During the fourteenth century, Charles IV revived the local viticultural industry by importing vines from Burgundy, and, stepping down in terraces from the castle, Mělník's vineyards are still famous, and the wine is on sale in the castle shop. The **zámek** (www.lobkowicz-melnik.cz; charge) is in a variety of styles ranging from Gothic to Baroque, and has interesting wine cellars. Nearby, the parish church with its landmark tower has a *kostnice* (ossuary).

Mělník

TEREZÍN AND LITOMĚŘICE

Within sight of each other, and only separated by the River Labe, the towns of **Terezín** ⑳ and **Litoměřice** could hardly be more different. For centuries the market centre for the fertile surrounding countryside, historic Litoměřice was one of Bohemia's most important settlements, with a vast central square and a wealth of churches. By contrast, Terezín is an ugly upstart, a grim fortress town of barrack blocks, laid out in the late eighteenth century to protect the northern approaches to Prague. Outside the main walls and moats, the **Small Fortress** (Malá pevnost; www.pamatnik-terezin.cz; charge) served as a political prison in Austro-Hungarian times. The regime was brutal, but nothing like what was to come under the Nazis. In 1941 they expelled all Terezín's inhabitants, and turned the town into what they claimed was a model ghetto. No extermination camp, Terezín nevertheless saw thousands of deaths, and a majority of those incarcerated here were eventually transported to Auschwitz. The **Ghetto Museum** brings home the horror of the place as well as celebrating the unquenchable spirit which made it a centre of creative endeavour, however temporary.

PILSEN

Only an hour away by train from the capital, Bohemia's second city has a couple of major attractions that draw tourists away from Prague's medieval splendour, at least for a day. Top billing here goes to the **Prazdroj (Urquell) Brewery** (www.prazdroj.cz/pro-navstevniky, charge), a short walk from the recently renovated main railway station. The fascinating tour tells the story of the world's first and finest Pils beer, shows off the brewing process and ends in the cellars with a tasting session of the Czechs' premium lager. The adjoining **Brewery Museum** is one of the best in the world.

Pilsen is home to the heavy engineering arm of Škoda, the city exporting trains and trams across the globe. One part of the massive industrial area to the west of the city centre has been turned into **Techmania Science Centre** (www.techmania.cz, charge), arguably the country's top attraction for children. Countless experiments, demonstrations and interactive exhibits involving laws of physics, chemistry and every other conceivable scientific discipline await, and there's a cheap lunch café on the premises. Count on spending the entire day here, especially if you visit the planetarium in the afternoon.

The Ossuary, Kutna Hora

Pilsen's main square is **náměstí Republiky**, a large open space dominated by the **Cathedral of St Bartholomew**, which has the tallest church spire in the Czech Republic.

KUTNÁ HORA

On high ground overlooking a winding river valley, this old town was at its peak in the Middle Ages, when it was bigger than London, and the silver extracted from its mines underpinned the prosperity of Prague and the Bohemian royal court. When the silver ran out, the town shrank to less than a third of its former size and became a provincial backwater. There is still plenty of evidence of **Kutná Hora**'s ⓸② glory days; enough to make it one of the most popular day trips from the capital. The outstanding monument is **St Barbara's Cathedral** (Chrám sv. Barbora; www.

chramsvatebarbory.cz; charge). Despite its incomplete state, this is one of the finest examples of Central European Gothic architecture. Begun at the end of the fourteenth century, in the mid-sixteenth century it was given its extraordinary roof by Benedikt Ried, who also designed the exquisite vaulting in the nave.

On one side of the street running north from the cathedral is the huge **Jesuit College**, on the other, above the drop to the river, a line of Baroque sculptures of gesticulating saints. Further along the valley rim, the fifteenth-century palace known as the **Hradek** contains the Czech Museum of Silver, while beyond rises the tower of another major church, **St James** (sv. Jakub).

Adjacent to the church is the restored powerhouse of the city's medieval economy, the **Italian Court** (Vlašský dvůr; www.pskh.cz; charge), which shelters a museum of minting. It was here that minting experts brought in from Florence turned out the Prague *groschen*, legal tender over much of the known world until the nineteenth century.

Konopiště castle

In the suburb of Sedlec just northeast of the town, next to a Gothic church given a Baroque makeover by the architect Santini, stands one of the country's great curiosities, the **Ossuary** (Kostnice; www.ossuary.eu; charge), containing a fantastical array of bells, coats of arms and chandeliers, all made from human bones.

PRŮHONICE

Almost a suburb of Prague, the village of **Průhonice** ❸ is famous for its UNESCO-listed castle and vast landscaped park. The castle (not normally open to the public) is occupied by the Botanical Institute of the National Academy of Science, whose botanists have a wonderful array of trees, shrubs and other plants at their disposal in the vast park where they work. Průhonice Castle dates to the Middle Ages, but the present building is a romantic structure in Czech neo-Renaissance style. It was built in the late nineteenth century by Count Ernst Silva-Taroucca, who was also responsible for laying out the park (www.pruhonickypark.cz; charge), a major achievement of landscape design, with lakes, vistas, walks, an alpine garden and, above all, countless trees, both native and exotic.

Český Šternberk towers over the Sázava Valley

KONOPIŠTĚ

The Czech Republic's main motorway connecting Prague to Brno and beyond leads beyond the communist-era outer suburbs into attractive countryside rich in parks and castles. Close to the town of Benešov rises **Konopiště** ❹ (www.zamek-konopiste.cz; charge), which almost rivals Karlštejn in popularity with visitors. Originally a medieval stronghold built in the thirteenth century, it was restored and modernised in the late nineteenth century by Archduke Franz Ferdinand. Redolent of the last days of the Austro-Hungarian Empire, the interiors seem much as they were lived in by the archduke and his family, while the pervasive decoration with hunting trophies reflects his passion for the chase. A particular highlight is the armoury, one of the finest private collections in the world. Franz Ferdinand re-landscaped the castle park, providing it with a lavish rose garden.

NOTES

Cold-shouldered at the imperial court in Vienna because he had married Sophie Chotek, a mere countess, Franz Ferdinand was happy to hide away in his rural retreat at Konopiště, where he is reckoned to have shot animals by the hundred thousand. He himself perished by the bullet, when he and Sophie were assassinated in Sarajevo in June 1914 by a Serb nationalist, in what is generally considered to be the starting signal for World War I.

ČESKÝ ŠTERNBERK

While Konopiště is buried deep in woodland, the castle at **Český Šternberk** 15 (www.hradceskysternberk.cz; charge) sits atop a rocky ridge high above the River Sázava, seemingly impregnable against all comers. The castle was begun in the mid-thirteenth century by a member of the Šternberk family, one of the most powerful dynasties in the realm. It has been greatly remodelled over the years and in its present form is a largely Baroque structure. Under communism, a Šternberk was allowed to stay on as curator, a quite incredible fact. Today, the restored stronghold is worth a visit for its superb views and its fascinating, often oddly shaped interiors. It is filled with furnishings and fittings in styles ranging from Renaissance to Empire, as well as portraits, hunting trophies, chandeliers and artefacts from the Thirty Years' War, when the castle survived a couple of sieges.

A performance by the
Prague State Opera Ballet

Things to do

Prague is bursting at the seams with things to do, even after the museums and galleries have shut. There's something for everyone in the Czech capital, from highbrow culture to noisy beer halls. The cost of a night out, whatever you choose to do, is refreshingly low.

CULTURE

Prague is home to a multitude of theatre, ballet and opera companies, with a strong tradition of puppetry and mime. However, it is undoubtedly in the field of classical music that it has established itself as a world leader, as its wealth of concert venues and its packed musical programme will testify.

MUSIC

The city has been a major concert venue for at least five centuries. It witnessed the premiere of Mozart's *Don Giovanni* and played

KAFKA: BACK IN THE LIMELIGHT

Like a great number of the central figures in the history of Prague, Franz Kafka spoke German. This factor lost him the support of the Czech public when the country rid itself once and for all of Austro-Hungarian state supervision in 1918, and again in 1945 when the German minority was expelled. The author of *The Castle, The Trial* and *Metamorphosis* was equally shunned by the communist regime for being a bourgeois intellectual.

But Kafka is firmly back in fashion. The Franz Kafka Museum (Cihelná 2b; www.kafkamuseum.cz) uses multimedia displays to explore the writer's background, emphasising the influence of personal experiences on his books. Other sights linked with the author's life such as Zlatá ulička (Golden Lane) at Prague Castle and the Generali building in Národní Avenue where Kafka worked can also be visited.

host to numerous world-leading composers during their careers. Large concert halls have been built during various periods in the history of Prague and today, along with a clutch of smaller venues, they provide a welcoming stage for concerts all year long.

The city is home to some very fine classical ensembles, foremost of which is the **Czech Philharmonic Orchestra** (www.ceskafilharmonie.cz), one of the best in the world. Others include the **Prague Symphony Orchestra** (www.fok.cz) and the **Prague Radio Symphony Orchestra** (www.socr.rozhlas.cz). These, and touring ensembles, appear at venues such as the **Rudolfinum** (www.rudolfinum.cz) or **Smetana Hall** at the Municipal House (www.obecnidum.cz). Lesser-known touring outfits or smaller groups, for example quartets, often perform at the **Clementinum** or **St Nicholas Church** to name a couple of venues.

Throughout the year, large-scale festivals devote themselves to the work of particular composers or specific musical styles. The best of these is the **Prague Spring** (www.festival.cz). Czech favourites such as Dvořák and Smetana feature heavily on the programme and hearing their music in their homeland is an experience not to be forgotten.

Concerts are held at lunchtime and in the evening and you can purchase seats online or through Prague's tourist offices. Alternatively, head to the box office of the venue in question. With ticket prices representing such good value, there is the potential to see a different performance each day – and many people do just that. Ticketmaster (www.ticketmaster.cz) is now the top ticket reseller.

THEATRE AND BALLET

The city is also home to the Czech National Theatre, ballet and opera companies, and regularly welcomes touring groups. The **National Theatre** (www.narodni-divadlo.cz) is an enormous complex with several stages, and encompasses the national opera and ballet companies. It also includes the **Laterna Magika**, a multimedia theatre that blends music, mime, ballet, surrealism and satire into a powerful melange that transcends the language barrier. Each season, the **Estates Theatre** (www.narodni-divadlo.cz) also plays host to several companies, and the **State Opera** (www.narodni-divadlo.cz) stages seminal opera, ballet and dance productions.

Czech puppetry has been designated a piece of UNESCO Intangible Cultural Heritage so catching a puppet performance here is not

Dvořák's works top the bill in Prague's concert halls

just for children. Shows take place at the **National Marionette Theatre** (www.mozart.cz). You can watch the puppets run the gamut of emotions in sophisticated plays of a more serious bent, or clown around in light-hearted pieces.

Useful listings of what's on during your stay in the city can be found on the website of the English-language *Prague Post* newspaper (www.praguepost.com) as well as on various Facebook groups.

NIGHTLIFE

If cultural overload strikes, why not seek refuge in Prague's plethora of bars and cafés where you can enjoy a few drinks and listen to live rock, jazz or folk music. For a glass of Prague's finest, head for one of the city's huge convivial beer cellars.

Prague's perfect stage set: the Charles Bridge at night

BEER HALLS AND COCKTAIL BARS

For well-kept beer and cosy surroundings try **U Hrocha** (Thunovská 10) and **U Kocoura** (Nerudova 2), both in Malá Strana, or the authentic **U Zlatého tygra** (Husova 17; www.uzlatehotygra.cz) and **U Medvidků** (Na Perštýně 7; www.umedvidku.cz) in the Old Town.

Perhaps surprisingly, Prague is also home to number of chic cocktail bars, including **Cloud 9** (*Hilton Prague*, Pobřežní 1; www.cloud9.cz) which offers breathtaking views over the city, **Bugsy's** (Pařížská 10; www.bugsysbar.cz), **Tretter's New York Bar** (V kolkovně 3; www.tretters.cz) and **Ocean Drive** (V kolkovně 7).

For something a little more earthy, Žižkov is famous for its pubs and the suitably loud and raucous **U vystřeleného oka** (U božích bojovníků 3; www.uvoka.cz) is the best drinking den to get a feel for the area.

CLUBS

As the evening wears on, Prague's lively nightlife kicks in. Trends can be short-lived, so keep an eye on the local press or websites such as www.techno.cz for the most popular club nights. For a relatively safe bet head for Prague's most long-standing club, **Radost FX** (Bělehradská 120; http://radostfx.cz). Still very stylish, this venue attracts the cream of the local DJs, not to mention international guest DJs, and holds a gay night once a week. Other places you might want to check out include the popular and well-dressed **Nebe** (V celnici 4); **Mecca** (U Průhonu 3; www.mecca.cz), which also holds jazz nights; and **Roxy** (Dlouhá 33; www.roxy.cz), popular for house and R&B.

While the Prague LGBTQ+ scene is fairly small there are some good venues to check out. The long-established mixed bar **Friends** (Bartolomějská 11; www.friendsclub.cz) is a good place to start, as is **21 Klub** (Římská 21; www.facebook.com/Klub21prague). Clubs to try include the mixed **TERmix** (Třebízského 4a; www.club-termix.cz) or the gay **Alcatraz** (Krakovská 19; http://mujalkac.webnode.cz).

Tretter's New York Bar

SHOPPING

The past three decades have seen huge changes in how and where people shop in the city. This is one area where Prague has completely broken away from its communist past of limited goods in state-owned department

Shoppers in the Old Town

stores. The city may still lag way behind other European capitals when it comes to retail but there are some worthwhile shops to check out in the historical centre.

The main shopping streets boast the flagship stores of all the well-known international chains though prices are higher than you might be used to back home. The Old Town has a smattering of small, specialist shops, some of them Czech-owned.

WHERE TO SHOP

The majority of the low-grade souvenir shops can be found along the Royal Way leading from Municipal House through the Old Town Square, and in Lesser Quarter Square across the river. Big names from the (Western) high street have set up shop around Wenceslas Square and along Na příkopě, whereas the more upmarket streets of Pařížská and Jungmannova see European haute couture rubbing shoulders with emerging Czech designer labels.

A good place to shop for souvenirs is the Týn Court (Týnský dvůr or Ungelt), just behind the Týn Church. Here you'll find books, clothes, wines to taste, and cafés and restaurants in which to take a break.

WHAT TO BUY

The Czech Republic has a reputation for the quality of its traditional products. **Glass** and porcelain are particularly good and examples of both are to be found in royal collections across Europe. **Moser**

Crystal is an exclusive brand name with a small factory in the spa town of Karlovy Vary and a shop in Prague. Its crystal comes in myriad shapes and patterns – prices are high. **Bohemia Crystal** is a traditional low-cost producer and its decanters, vases, bowls and glasses, with patterns cut by hand, make pretty souvenirs or gifts and are roughly half the price of similar items in other European countries.

More modern designs in glass are also popular, from large, decorative sculptures to vases. Bunches of large glass flowers mimic the shape of fresh blooms.

The delicate features of Bohemian **porcelain** figurines have changed little in the past two hundred years, and their flowing forms are highly prized among collectors. The best originate from small factories around Karlovy Vary, but they can also be bought in Prague.

A shop window in the Old Town sparkles crystal

Cubist replica furniture at Kubista

Thun and Pirkenhammer are two brands to look out for; the latter made the dinner services for the doomed liner RMS *Titanic*.

Prague has a reputation as being a **city of the arts**. There are numerous stalls selling – often rather low-quality – watercolours or line drawings of Prague. Moody black-and-white photographs offer yet another perspective of the city. Apart from these more obvious offerings, Prague also has several galleries selling works by both established and up-and-coming artists. For something out of the ordinary, look at the Cubist and Modernist replicas on sale at the **Kubista** (www.kubista.cz) and **Modernista** (www.modernista. cz) shops.

There are also many **antiques dealers**, with glass and porcelain being particularly prevalent. As a leading city of the Habsburg Empire, Prague counted a large number of wealthy and cosmopolitan citizens. These collections, along with a rich legacy of Bohemian furniture and artefacts, form the basis of today's trade in antiques.

Garnets have been mined and polished in the Czech Republic for centuries, and the pretty semiprecious stones can be bought in jewellery shops across the city. Those sold by the **Granát** shops are guaranteed to be the real Czech deal; they also sell genuine Vltavín (Moldavite) stones from South Bohemia.

Shops selling **Czech handicrafts** (try Manufaktura; www.manufaktura.cz) are often enticingly set in historic houses or converted cellars. Wooden **toys** make good presents for young children. **Ceramics** come in a variety of shapes and sizes, decorated with glazes made of earth pigments. In the Czech Republic, **decorated eggs** feature prominently in Easter celebrations and are widely available as souvenirs – coloured ribbons are attached so that you can hang them in your home. **Puppets** make an original memento and come in a range of characters. Finally, **basketwear** can be excellent although, unfortunately, the most beautiful items are often the largest and too bulky for the return flight home.

In a city that prides itself on its classical **music** heritage, it comes as no surprise that music is readily available, with some stores selling a huge range of classical recordings. Vinyl shops have made a big comeback in recent years.

Bottles of the Czech **beer** are perhaps too heavy to take home, but try a bottle of the heady Becherovka liqueur. Plum brandy or *slivovice* is also widely available, as are brandies distilled from other fruits.

SPORTS AND ACTIVITIES

Sparta Praha has traditionally been the Czech Republic's top **football** team. They play in a quite modest stadium (www.sparta.cz) adjacent to Letná Park and their season runs from July to April. **Ice hockey** is extremely popular, the main venue being HC Slavia's O2 Arena stadium (www.o2arena.cz). The Czechs are naturally proud of the number of professional **tennis** players they have produced

RIDES AND CRUISES

Apart from walking there are a variety of different ways of seeing the city. Old Tow tours in an open-top vintage car are a highlight, departing from the Old Town Square. Horse-drawn carriages were banned in 2023 after concerns about animal welfare.

Riverboats operating day or evening cruises ply the waters of the Vltava, with candlelit dinners or lunchtime buffets. It's a great way to see the sights that line the riverbanks and check out the islands studding the Vltava that tourists largely ignore. **Prague Boats** (www.prague-boats.cz) is the best company for cruises as it has the most modern vessels and best service, though there are several other operators. Prague Boats moors its cruisers on Dvořákovo Embankment just north of the Rudolfinum.

During the peak months (late March to mid-November, weekends and holidays), Prague's historic tram No 41 (www.dpp.cz) trundles around the city. The National Theatre, Malostranské náměstí and Wenceslas Square are all boarding points. Ordinary public transport tickets are not valid on this service.

in recent decades; Kateřina Siniaková and Tomáš Macháč won gold in the mixed doubles at the Paris 2024 Olympics (canoeists Martin Fuksa and Josef Dostál also scored gold in their disciplines). The National Tennis facility (www.cltk.cz) on Štvanice Island below the Hlávkův Bridge hosts Grand Prix tournaments.

There are a number of **swimming** pools in Prague. Plavecký stadion Podolí (Podolská 74; www.pspodoli.cz) is the largest complex in the city with two outdoor pools, one indoor, diving boards and a waterslide. Aquapalace Praha (Pražská 138; www.aquapalace.cz) in Průhonice is the largest water park in the country with myriad attractions, saunas, slides and eateries.

CHILDREN'S PRAGUE

At first glance Prague appears to have little to offer children, the accent of a typical tour being on visiting the major churches, palaces, galleries and beer halls. However, there are a few fun activities that will keep kids happy and maybe even amuse parents.

Transport can be entertaining: boat trips on the Vltava are fun, a simple ride on a tram can be a great experience in itself, and taking the funicular railway up to Petřín Hill thrills young ones.

With a little advance planning, a well-chosen **theatre trip** can be a stimulating experience even for small children. The Lanterna Magika features dance, mime and the use of lighting effects. The National Marionette Theatre (www.mozart.cz) stages shows for all ages, including a puppet version of *Don Giovanni*. If your child is mad about **funfairs**, a large one comes to the Prague Exhibition Ground during the summer months. Child-friendly **museums** include the National Technical Museum, with plenty of interactive

Boats on the Vltava

One of Prague's numerous puppet theatres

displays. The National Museum has collections of tropical insects and animal bones – children might be enthralled by the giant insects. Time your visit to Prague Castle to coincide with the hourly changing of the guards in the first courtyard – most impressive at noon. Prague has many green spaces, ideal for summer picnics.

Kids love the **Mirror Maze** on Petřin Hill, although younger children may find it frightening. Bite-sized lunchtime **concerts**, held at venues across town, can be a great way of introducing kids to classical music.

FESTIVALS AND EVENTS

Prague's cultural calendar is extremely busy and ever-changing, though even locals admit it is light on major festivals. Thise tend to be held in provincial towns and cities that aren't as clogged up with tourists. The following is a list some of the major annual events taking place both in the city and across the country. For up-to-date listings and information, the *Prague Post* is the best source.

May Prague International Marathon (dates vary from year to year).

May–June Prague Spring Festival (Pražské jaro; www.festival.cz), one of the world's best classical-music events, with performances by celebrated musicians at major venues throughout the city.

June Smetana's Litomyšl Festival (Litomyšl; www.smetano-valitomysl.cz), a celebration of classical music. Festival of the Five-petalled Rose (www.slavnostipetilisteruze.eu), a huge extravaganza of medieval dancing and music, fire-throwing and sword fights in Český Krumlov. Tanec Praha Contemporary Dance Festival (www.tanecpraha.cz), where foreign and Czech dancers collaborate. Rock for People Festival, a raucous affair of open-field music concerts (Hradec Králové; www.rockforpeople.cz).

July International Film Festival (Karlovy Vary; www.kviff.com). Summer Festivities of Early Music (www.letnislavnosti.cz).

July–August Prague Shakespeare Festival (www.shakespeare.cz), an ode to the great man with performances of Shakespearean plays at mainly open-air venues in the capital.

August Chopin Music Festival (www.chopinfestival.cz), an atmospheric summer music event held in the beautiful spa town of Mariánské Lázně (Marienbad).

September Wine festivals take place in Karlštejn, Mělník and across South Moravia.

October Signal Festival (www.signalfestival.com), a videomapping event with many after-dark projections around the capital.

November Prague Writers' Festival (www.pwf.cz), a literary affair with fascinating talks and book signings by internationally renowned authors.

December Advent and Christmas-time activities such as craft markets, carol concerts and an open-air arts festival.

31 December Spectacular New Year celebrations across the city.

Food and drink

Despite not being one of Europe's well-known cuisines, the Czech Republic's food culture often ends up pleasantly surprising visitors. Traditional Czech cooking uses down-to-earth ingredients, often seasonal, to create filling and tasty dishes. Although typically heavy with pork, dumplings, pickles and cream, lighter versions of classic Czech recipes can often be found. Beware though, portion sizes are usually huge.

Of course, with so many international visitors in Prague, an ever-growing crop of restaurants serving diverse cuisines have sprung up across the streets. In recent years Vietnamese cuisine has become very popular, largely down to the fact that the Czech

Inside one of Prague's many kavárny (cafés)

Republic has a huge Vietnamese expat community. Ukrainian food is now widely available, and Prague now has every type of cooking going, from Mexican to Pakistani, Serb to Japanese.

Even vegetarians and vegans won't go hungry these days, though in ordinary Czech restaurants you might be limited to two or three 'meat-free' options.

TOP 10 CZECH FOODS TO TRY

1. PORK KNUCKLE
Ubiquitous in all Prague's restaurants, this chunk of pork is often served with dumplings and sauerkraut.

2. FRIED CHEESE
Vegetarians usually become quickly acquainted with deep-fried, breadcrumbed edam as it is sometimes the only meat-free dish on menus. Typically accompanied by tartare sauce and chips or boiled potatoes.

3. SVÍČKOVÁ
Czech sirloin roast is drizzled with an almost-sweet vegetable sauce and paired with a generous serving of dumplings, whipped cream and cranberry sauce.

4. FRUIT DUMPLINGS
Fruit-filled dumplings swimming in melted butter and cream and sprinkled with poppy seeds, icing sugar and hard cottage cheese – heaven on a plate if you can find it.

5. GOULASH
Beef is usually the meat in this rich stew studded with dumplings and raw onion, but the venison version, typical for the Carlsbad Region, is better if you have the option.

6. CZECH WINE

Moravian wine doesn't find its way out of the country, so oeno-philes are sure to discover something new in the city's wine bars.

7. CHLEBÍČKY

These open sandwiches are piled high with toppings of ham, salami, egg, pickles and mayonnaise.

8. BEER

As of 2024 there were 435 breweries in the Czech lands. Most of them produce several types of beer meaning you really are spoilt for choice.

9. KOLÁČ

These traditional tarts are stuffed with poppy seeds, cottage cheese, jam and nut paste.

WHERE TO EAT

Restaurace. A restaurant but can be anything from a pub to a Michelin-starred establishment.

Hospoda. A pub, and most of them serve food.

Vinárny. Restaurant but with a focus on wine. Not as common as they once were.

Pivnice. A beer hall where the frothy tankards are the focus, the food an afterthought.

Kavárna. A coffee shop where cakes, pastries and sandwiches might also be served.

Cukrárna. The traditional Czech café-bakery was once ubiqui-tous in Prague but has been chased out of the city centre. Serves everything from Austrian-style pastries to shots of vodka.

Jídelna. Cheap, basic canteens where many Czechs still head for lunch. Surprisingly, several have survived and thrive in the city centre.

Traditional Czech cooking uses down-to-earth ingredients

10. ROAST PORK

The tender meat served with sauerkraut and dumplings is officially the Czech national dish.

EATING OUT

On weekdays, most Czechs eat early – generally at around 7pm – then head to bed in preparation for the traditionally very early start to the working day ahead. However, restaurants in Prague stay open until around 10pm or 11pm, and even later at weekends, when locals go out to party.

Most restaurants post a printed menu *(jídelní lístek)* near the door, giving you at least an idea of their prices. Rare is the Prague eatery that doesn't have menus in English and German as well as Czech and perhaps other languages such as Korean and Chinese.

A menu might be divided into the following categories: *studená jídla* (cold dishes), *polévky* (soups), *teplé předkrmy* (warm starters), *ryby* (fish), *drůbež* (poultry), *hotová jídla* (main courses), and *moučníky* (desserts). A growing number of establishments are offering set meals at lunchtime and in the evening in addition to à la carte.

STARTERS AND SOUPS

Try a starter of Prague ham (*Pražská šunka*), a succulent local special-ity. It might come served in thin slices, garnished with cucumber and horseradish; with cheese in miniature sandwiches; or folded into horns and stuffed with cream or cream cheese and horseradish.

Soup is a popular choice at both lunch *(oběd)* and dinner *(večeře)*. Either a fairly light bouillon or, as is more likely, a thick,

A traditional restaurant in Nové Město

wholesome soup of pota-toes, vegetables and per-haps some meat. One of the heartiest traditional recipes is *bramborová polévka s houbami*, potato soup with mushrooms, flavoured with onion, bacon, carrots, cab-bage, parsley and spices – almost a meal in itself.

MEATY MAINS

The hearty Czech cuisine typically centres on well-roasted pork or beef with thick gravy. This is supple-mented with poultry, game or fish dishes – owing to the tradition of seasonal hunting in the surrounding

WHEN TO EAT

Breakfast (snídaně). The first meal of the day is served by hotels from about 6am to 10.30am and is usually in the form of a buffet, its lavishness depending on the class of the hotel. There will always be tea and coffee, a choice of cereals, cold meats, cheese, eggs, yoghurt and fruit. Check whether the price of breakfast is included in the room rate.

Lunch (oběd). For Czech office workers this is the main meal of the day, which is good news for tourists as almost every Prague eatery has a cheap lunch menu (around 150–200Kč).

Dinner (Večeře). For Czechs a light affair; for tourists often the main sit-down meal of the day.

countryside. Depending on the time of year, you might find duck, goose, boar and venison on the menu. The filling savoury food goes down best with cold Czech beer. For a taste of the Austro-Hungarian Empire, you should order *smažený řízek* (Wiener schnitzel), a delicious breaded veal escalope.

As an accompaniment, pride of place goes to the dumpling. Either made from bread (*houskové knedlíky*, relatively light) or potato (*bramborové knedlíky*, heavier in texture) you will usually find one or two sliced dumplings on your plate. Vegetables have always played a secondary role in traditional cuisine, and when they do appear in soups and stews can seem overcooked. You will often see 'stewed vegetables' on menus in English, which forewarns you that they will definitely not be arriving *al dente*. Sauerkraut (*kyselé zelí*) is a popular side – red or white cabbage cooked to a melting consistency in animal fat, sugar and a little vinegar.

DESSERTS

Desserts usually figure in the heavyweight category, for example the tasty *jablkový závin* (apple strudel), topped with whipped cream. *Svestkové knedlíky* (plum dumplings) are sprinkled with

┌─ **ETIQUETTE** ─────────────────────────────────

In restaurants, waiters hand out menus and are usually back within a few minutes to take drinks orders. When ordering main dishes, sides are usually ordered separately. In the presence of locals, the custom is to say a hearty *'dobrou chuť* (the equivalent of bon appetit) before starting to eat. Tipping usually involves rounding the bill up to the nearest 100Kč. Never click your fingers to attract a waiter's attention – this is regarded as rude and will lead to you potentially being ignored for the rest of the evening. Asking for tap water will usually meet with bewilderment and your request will most certainly be turned down – Czechs don't drink it. Order mineral water instead.

└──

cheese curd and sugar, and then doused in melted butter. A firm favourite is *palačinka*, ice cream or cream and fruit enveloped in a pancake. Finally, *zmrzlina* (ice cream) or *kompot* (stewed fruit) – sometimes laced with fruit brandy – are old standbys.

VEGETARIAN DISHES

The presence of a large expatriate community has led to the emergence of several vegetarian cafés and restaurants over the past few years. Consequently, many non-vegetarian restaurants now offer a range of options *bezmasá jídla* (meat-free dishes). The Dhaba Beas chain (www.dhababeas.cz), which has branches across the city, offers a delicious vegetarian buffet where you pay by weight.

STREET FOOD

Prague once had a thriving street food scene, but its popularity has severely waned in the past two decades. If you can find it, top billing goes to the *bramborák*, an oily, garlicky potato pancake, delicious and filling despite the greasy fingers. *Pečená klobása* (roasted sausage) on a paper plate, with a slice of rye bread and a squirt of mild mustard is a great way to stave off the munchies at 4am. *Párek v rohlíku* is a pork hotdog in the staple bread roll adorned with a streak of ketchup or mustard. American-style fast-food outlets are plentiful, particularly around Wenceslas Square, and are now more popular with young Czechs than the traditional snack outlets. Soft ice cream is popular with Czechs and so can be found everywhere and is still very cheap by Western standards. Gelato-style ice cream never caught on with locals but is widely available where tourists go.

DRINKS

Prague offers a wonderful selection of places to drink, many of which also serve light meals, and its architectural wealth ensures a range of superb settings. In addition to this, the city has witnessed a renaissance of the thriving café society of the early twentieth century.

The Czechs love their pork

Czech beer has a reputation to be envied

Czech beer *(pivo)* has a reputation to be envied, and the
city of Plzeň (Pilsen) has given
the world the *pilsner* style of
lager, imitated by most other
countries. Naturally, locals
are adamant that no other
beer tastes quite the same
because the distinctive fla-
vour of Czech beer comes
from the pure water and the
excellence of its hops, which
grow on vast wood-and-
wire frames west of Prague.

┌─ THE ART OF DRINKING ──────────

Beer halls are a veritable institution in Bohemia, so much so that some unwritten rules of conduct have evolved over the centuries. Once you take a seat, the waiter will assume you are there for the beer and will plonk a pint down in front of you; when you are almost finished, another is likely to arrive without you saying a word. Always use beer mats, and never complain that your beer has too much of a head – in this country that's a sign the beer is fresh. Sharing a table with strangers is perfectly acceptable, as is moving chairs around, but not tables. Round up the bill to the nearest 100Kč as a tip, but never reward bad service.

west of Prague. The most famous beers are *Pilsner Urquell* from Plzeň, Budweiser *Budvar* from České Budějovice (Budweis) and *Staropramen* from Prague. Other well-regarded breweries abound in Prague and the smaller surrounding towns. Several pubs brew their own light *(světle)* or dark *(tmave)* blends, including U Fleků which has been in operation since 1499. All Czech beer is tasty and refreshing but it might be wise to bear in mind that it is probably stronger than what you are used to drinking at home.

A fairly recent development is the emergence of non-alcoholic beers. Birell from the Urquell Brewery in Pilsen is the best known. However, Bakalář non-alcoholic beer from Rakovník is regarded as the best in the world, though it's usually only available in bottles.

Some Czech wine *(víno)* is excellent and novelty wines such as ice wine (wine made from frozen grapes) and hay wine (wine made from grapes dried in hay) are worth seeking out. However, Czechs' wine consumption is way under the EU average and it's usually best to stick to beer outside gourmet establishments. White is *bílé* and red is *červené*. A drink local to Karlovy Vary, *becherovka* is made of herbs and served chilled as an aperitif, as is the powerful, sweetish *stará myslivecká*. After-dinner drinks generally take the form of fruit brandies, especially *slivovice* which is made from plums.

TO HELP YOU ORDER

May I see the menu? **Mohu vidět jídelní lístek?**
Can I have it without...? **Mohu mít bez...?**
I am a vegetarian. **Jsem vegeterián(ka).** (m/f)
The bill, please. **Zaplatím.**
I'd like… **Prosím…**

beer **pivo**	meat **maso**
bread **chléb**	the menu **jídelní lístek**
butter **máslo**	milk **mléko**
cheese **sýr**	mineral water **minerálku**
coffee **kávu**	salad **salát**
dessert **moučník**	sugar **cukr**
egg **vejce**	tea **čaj**
ice cream **zmrzlinu**	wine **víno**

MENU READER

bažant pheasant	**klobása** sausage
brambory potatoes	**knedlíky** dumplings
drůbež poultry	**králík** rabbit
fazole beans	**kuře** chicken
houby mushrooms	**květák** cauliflower
hovězí beef	**kyselé zelí** sauerkraut
hrášek peas	**pstruh** trout
hrozny grapes	**rajčata** tomatoes
hrušky pears	**rýže** rice
husa goose	**špenát** spinach
jablka apples	**srnčí/jelení/dančí** venison
jahody strawberries	**štika** pike
játra liver	**šunka** ham
jazyk tongue	**švestky** plums
jehněčí lamb	**telecí** veal
kachna duck	**vepřové** pork
kapr carp	**žebírka** ribs

Places to eat

Each restaurant and café reviewed in this Guide is accompanied by a price category, based on the cost of a three-course meal (or similar) for one.

€€€€€ = over Kč1000 (over €40)
€€€€ = Kč700–1000 (€28–€40)
€€€ = Kč500–700 (€20–€28)
€€ = Kč300–500 (€12–€20)
€ = under Kč300 (Under €12)

OLD TOWN AND NEW TOWN

Bílá Kráva Rubešova 10, www.bilakrava.cz. On a quiet street tucked behind the National Museum, the 'White Cow' owes its name to the occupation of its owner, who moonlights as a cattle farmer in Burgundy, France. Most of the dishes use meat from his herd, flown directly into Prague, but a variety of seafood and lamb dishes also have their place on the dining table. A cosy wood-beamed, cottage-like interior complements an ambitious menu that ranges from *escargots* in red wine to *bœuf bourguignon*. €€€€

Café Slavia Smetanovo nábřeží 1012/2, www.cafeslavia.cz. Prague's most famous café occupies the corner opposite the National Theatre. A swish Art Deco interior, an imaginative globally influenced menu, excellent coffee and cocktails, and an olde-worlde atmosphere make this a must-see and a tourist attraction in its own right. Great place for a pre-show drink or a rainy afternoon with a book as you watch the trams rattle by. €€€

Červený jelen Hybernská 1034/5, www.cervenyjelen.cz. Huge, modern restaurant near Masaryk railway station in the New Town serving a meat-heavy menu and Pilsen beer by the hectolitre. The contemporary dining space must have the highest ceiling of any eatery in Central Europe. €€

Cicala Žitná 43, www.trattoria.cz. A basement trattoria set off a busy street that runs east from the top end of Charles Square, *Cicala* serves some of the most authentic and tasty Italian food in the city. The menu offers antipasti, pasta and meat dishes, plus daily specials. €€€

Country Life Melantrichova 15, www.countrylife.cz. Tucked away in a small street leading south off Old Town Square, this self-service vegetarian eatery was the first meat-free restaurant in the capital. It is one of the few places in the city centre that also offers vegan dishes and there's a health-food store next door. €€

Ginger & Fred Tančící dům, Jiráskovo náměstí 6, www.gfrest.cz. Located on the top floor of one of Prague's most famous modern landmarks, Frank Gehry's 'dancing' or 'Fred and Ginger' building – so-called because of its flowing forms – offers sweeping views of the city from both the dining room and the rooftop terrace. The menu of international cuisine changes with the seasons. €€€€€

Havelská Koruna Havelská 23, www.havelska-koruna.cz. One of the cheapest eats in Prague, this large self-service canteen has an extensive menu of no-nonsense Czech staples, dessert counter and fierce, ladle-wielding dinner ladies. Great place for an inexpensive refuel in the New Town. €

Jídelna Světozor Vodičkova 39, www.jidelnasvetozor.webnode.cz. Right at the heart of Prague city centre is one of the most affordable places to dine in town. Located in the Světozor Arcade, this self-service canteen plates up the basics of Czech cuisine for a few crowns and is popular with local office workers. €

Kolkovna Celnice V Celnici 1031/4, www.kolkovna.cz. Just off náměstí Republiky, this Pilsner Urquell-owned beer hall pairs excellent beer with hearty Bohemian food. It also has the advantage of being on top of one of Prague's best clubs, where you can dance off the dumplings. €€

King Solomon Široká 8, www.kosher.cz. Fittingly right in the middle of the Jewish Quarter is the only strictly kosher restaurant in Prague with Hebrew-speaking staff. Among the classic dishes of Central European Jewish cooking are chicken soup, gefilte fish, carp with prunes and duckling drumsticks with schollet and sautéed cabbage. Kosher wines are imported from Israel, Hungary and France, as well as offering some Czech bottles. It is possible to arrange Shabbat meals beforehand and to have them delivered to your hotel. **€€€€€**

Kogo Na Příkopě 22, www.kogo.cz. A large, bustling and very popular Mediterranean-style eatery in the Slovanský Dům arcade on Prague's main shopping street, with a range of fish, meat, and pasta dishes. **€€€€**

Kogo Havelská Havelská 499/27, http://kogohavelska.cz. A relaxed but upmarket Italian restaurant and pizzeria not far from Staroměstské náměstí. It offers the full range of Italian cuisine, with enticing starters and desserts. Breakfast menu also available. Booking is recommended. **€€€€**

Las Adelitas Malé náměstí, www.lasadelitas.cz. Possibly the best Mexican food in Central and Eastern Europe is served up across Prague by this chain helmed by authentic Mexican chefs. This branch has a superb location between the Old Town Square and Charles Bridge and plates up enchiladas, tacos and quesadillas to die for. **€€€**

Lehká Hlava Boršov 280/2, www.lehkahlava.cz. Considered by some as Prague's best vegetarian restaurant, this long-established place has a weird-and-wonderful interior designed by local artists, a lively vibe and internationally inspired mains such as Thai red curry and meat-free burritos. Just a few steps from Charles Bridge, the backstreet location is refreshingly quiet. **€€€**

Lokal Dlouháááá Dlouhá 33, http://lokal-dlouha.ambi.cz. In the heart of the Old Town, this friendly beer hall serves traditional, home-made Czech fare at reasonable prices. You can also learn how to draw beer from the bartenders; the courses are held in Czech and English. €€

Mlynec Novotného lávka 9, www.mlynec.cz. In a beautiful location by the river, with views of the Charles Bridge. The degustation menu at this upmarket place featuring dishes such as *coquilles St-Jacques*, oxtail consommé and saddle of deer is well worth trying. €€€€

Mincovna Staroměstské náměstí 930/7, www.restauracemincovna.cz. Most of the restaurants that spill out onto the Old Town Square are tourist traps and best avoided, but there are a couple of exceptions and 'The Mint' is one of them. Escape the tourist crush to enter a surprisingly low-key design space where you can enjoy a meat-rich menu for relatively reasonable prices for the location. Serves Pilsen beers. €€

Svatováclavská cukrárna Václavská pasáž, Karlovo náměstí. One of the last genuine *cukrárnas* (traditional Czech café-bakery) remaining in the city centre, this always-packed place in an interwar shopping arcade just off Karlovo náměstí serves up a wealth of cakes, pastries, open sandwiches, coffees, wine and much more. A great place to people-watch and hang out with a Turkish coffee and wedge of cheap strudel. €

Ungelt Restaurant Týn 638/5, www.restaurant-ungelt.cz. Tucked away in the charming surroundings of the cobbled Týn Court, behind the Týn Church, the *Ungelt Restaurant* serves primarily fish, but also a variety of meat and vegetarian dishes. The menu is accompanied by an excellent wine list. An outdoor terrace makes a pretty setting for summertime dining. €€€€€

U Šumavy Štěpánská 543/3, www.usumavy.cz. A little piece of the Czech countryside transported to downtown Prague, *U Šumavy* has a no-nonsense menu of Bohemian favourites, well-kept lager and a pretty wood-panelled dining room to enjoy it all in. €€

La Veranda Elišky Krásnohorské 2, Prague 1, www.laveranda.cz. A gourmet restaurant near the Spanish Synagogue, *La Veranda* is a light, stylish venue filled with flowers. It specialises in delicate fish dishes but has good meat and vegetarian options too. Cooking styles range from Mediterranean to Asian fusion. Excellent service and above-average prices, but certainly worth the splurge. **€€€€**

CASTLE, MALÁ STRANA & AROUND

Café Savoy Vítězná 5, http://cafesavoy.ambi.cz. This Austro Hungarian-era café in the south corner of the Lesser Quarter, just by the western end of the Legií Bridge, is a good place to stop for refreshment. Choose between excellent French-inspired gourmet food, the café menu or the home-made cakes beneath a beautifully restored neo-Renaissance ceiling. **€€€**

Coda Tržiště 9, www.codarestaurant.cz. Set in the *Aria Hotel*, this smart restaurant has a rooftop terrace offering spectacular views of the Lesser Town and the castle. Beautiful interiors were designed by two Italian architects Rocco Magnoli and Lorenzo Carmellini. It has a good degustation menu of Czech cuisine with traditional *kulajda* soup, roasted duck and plum ravioli, prepared by the head chef Igor Chramec. **€€€€**

Cukrkavalimonáda Lázeňská 7, http://cukrkavalimonada.com. On a little square just to the south of Mostecká, 'Sugar-coffee-lemonade' is a beautifully styled café offering variations around scrambled eggs for breakfast, then pastas, frittatas, pancakes and sandwiches throughout the day, followed by Mediterranean-style meals come early evening. Try the home-made pastries and cakes. **€€**

Czech Slovak Foodery Újezd 20, www.foodery.czechslovak.cz. Located on busy Újezd near the lower station of the Petřín funicular, this modern restaurant seeks to resurrect the traditional dishes of the Czechs' and Slovaks' forefathers. This includes excellent goulash in beer, *halušky* (dumplings) from Slovakia and grilled meats. A little pricey, but the food is excellent and well presented. €€€€

Dhaba Beas Viktora Huga 1, www.dhababeas.cz. This vegetarian chain canteen has branches all over the city and beyond. Take a metal tray, pile it high with meat-free treats, add a free water or tea and pay by the weight of the food. This branch in the Smíchov district is a tranquil tourist-free haven. Despite being a chain, all the branches are different in design. €

Kampa Park Na Kampě 8b, www.kampagroup.com. This well-established Czech restaurant on Kampa Island near Charles Bridge is extremely popular – and not just because of its magnificent setting. Its creative international fare, including mouth-watering fish and seafood, is just as enticing. The extensive wine list features over 150 wines. The riverside terrace is particularly attractive. €€€€€

Kuchyň Hradčanské náměstí 186/1, www.kuchyn.ambi.cz. Right opposite the castle gates, this understandably pricey restaurant has some of the finest views of any Prague eatery – essentially of the whole of the city unfurling beneath the promontory on which the castle sits. The superbly executed food is an imaginative twist on Czech country fare. €€€€

Lidová Jídelna Těšnov 5, www.lidovajidelna.cz. Travel back in time to the days of the socialist utopia at the lunch-only 'People's Canteen' in the unfashionable Těšnov neighbourhood. The food is basic Czech fare, the prices are low, and the diners mainly local workers. €

U Malířů 1543 Maltézské náměstí 11, www.umaliru1543.com. This restaurant is one the most expensive in Prague, found on a quiet square in the Lesser Quarter, just to the east of Karmelitská. French *haute cuisine* is served in a beautiful sixteenth-century dining room complete with an elaborately decorated ceiling. A tiny outdoor terrace completes the picture. Absolutely perfect for a special occasion. €€€€€

U Modré kachničky Nebovidská 460/6, www.umodrekachnicky.cz. 'At the Blue Duckling' is a popular restaurant near Maltézské náměstí, featuring Art Nouveau images on the walls, acres of dark wood and a smattering of overstuffed chairs. Traditional Czech cuisine dominates the menu, as does plenty of game and fish. €€€

U Raka Černínská 93, www.hoteluraka.cz. This surprisingly bucolic hotel at the western end of Nový Svět has a small café serving light meals. €€€

Monastiq Nebovidská 459/1, www.mandarinoriental.com. Head chef at the *Mandarin Oriental Hotel*, Michal Horváth produces light, imaginative versions of Czech dishes, enjoyed in an intimate, vaulted dining room. There's also a beautiful, curtained terrace for those humid summer Prague nights. €€€€

Terasa U Zlate Studne U Zlaté studně 166/4, www.terasauzlatestudne. cz. Poised on the roof of the *Golden Well* hotel, just a stone's throw from Lesser Town square, this elegant restaurant offers panoramic views of Vltava River and the spires of the Old Town – ideal for a romantic dinner. The acclaimed chef Pavel Sapic prepares a wonderful range of international dishes. There is a good list of international and Czech wines. €€€€€

U Knoflíčků Újezd 412/17, www.uknoflicku.cz. A pretty slice of classic Czech amid the international tourist scene, this traditional café-bakery is a wonderful place to linger over open sandwiches, cakes and coffee for under 150Kč or to spend a lazy afternoon watching the world go by on bustling Újezd. €

Vegan's Prague Nerudova 36, www.vegansprague.cz. Arguably the best vegan restaurant in Prague, this is an excellent lunch stop on the way to the castle. In the modern beamed dining room, diners feast on plates of meat- and dairy-free meals, including Czech classics that usually contain huge wedges of pork. Great for non-vegans, too. €€€

Travel essentials

PRACTICAL INFORMATION

ACCESSIBLE TRAVEL

Accessibility in the Czech Republic has some way to go before it reaches Western standards, although attitudes are changing and EU legislation has been put in place. Transport is a major problem. Buses and old trams are inaccessible for wheelchairs, though many metro stations are now accessible, and the two train stations (Hlavní nádraží and nádraží Holešovice) have self-operating lifts. Prague's cobbles and general lack of ramps also make life hard on the streets. For a list of wheelchair-friendly hotels, restaurants, metro stations and so forth, order the various specialised guidebooks published by the Prague Wheelchair Association (Pražská organizace vozíčkářů), Benediktská 6, Staré Město (www.pov.cz). The association can organise an airport pick-up if you contact it well in advance, and can help with transporting wheelchairs.

ACCOMMODATION

Prague has many large hotels, but very few old-world, family-run establishments. Most hotels dating from the communist era have very dour exteriors, although many have been renovated, bringing the facilities and interiors up to international standards. A few gems from the city's glorious Art Nouveau era have also been refurbished and there are now many new luxury design and boutique hotels. Short-term rental sites such as Airbnb operate in the city centre.

I'd like a single room/double room **Chtěl bych jednolůžkový pokoj/dvoulůžkový pokoj.**
with bath/with shower **s koupelnou/se sprchou**
What's the rate per day? **Kolik stojí za den?**

AIRPORT

Václav Havel Airport Prague (www.prg.aero/en) is situated ten kilometres (6.5 miles) northwest of the city. Airport express bus (AE) operated by the public transport authority (www.dpp.cz) runs between the airport and the main railway station in the city centre every fifteen to thirty minutes from 5am–10.30pm. The journey takes about half-hour to Hlavní Nádraži (100Kč). Tickets can be bought from the driver. A cheaper (40Kč) but lengthier option is trolleybus No. 59 to the metro station Nádraží Veleslavín, then metro line A to the centre, or bus No. 100 to the metro line B at Zličín. Buy tickets in the terminal or from the machine at the bus stop. To take a taxi from the airport, use the Uber terminal at arrivals.

APPS

Download the **PID** app to navigate the city's public transport network, buy tickets and passes, and find your best route and nearest stop; handy filters include wheelchair-accessible. Cyclists and hikers might prefer **mapy.cz**, which details safe cycling routes and marked walking paths. Looking for an expertly brewed speciality coffee along the way? Download **European Coffee Trip** to discover your nearest artisan coffeeshop.

BICYCLE RENTAL

While some parts of Prague are quite hilly, hiring a bike to get around can be fun and convenient. Contact **Praha Bike** (www.prahabike.cz).

BUDGETING FOR YOUR TRIP

Due to the strength of the *koruna* Prague is no longer a particularly cheap destination for visitors from countries that use the euro, pound or dollar.

Hotel: Mid-range hotel per room per night Kč4,000–5,000.

Meals and drinks: Large glass of beer Kč50–100; three-course dinner per person Kč400–9000; soft drink Kč70.

Entertainment: Theatre tickets Kč400–1,000 with state company, or international performances from Kč1,200. Concert tickets are Kč200–600.

Tours: City walking tour (3hr) Kč6000.

CAMPING

A large campsite on the banks of the Vltava, **Autocamp Trojská** (Trojská 375/157, Prague 7; www.autocamp-trojska.cz), not far from Troja Palace and the zoo, is the closest to the centre. The Prague Information Service (tel: 12 444; www.prague.eu) has details of other campsites.

CAR HIRE

If you plan to stay in the city rather than touring the countryside, a car is more trouble than it is worth. If you do want to hire a vehicle, major international firms operate at Prague Airport.

Drivers must be at least 21 years of age and have held a full driving licence for one year. The daily hire charge for a medium-sized car (by European standards) is around Kč2,000–3,500 per day with unlimited mileage.

I'd like to rent a car. **Chtěl bych si půjčit auto**
large/small **velké/malé**
for one day/a week **na jeden den/týden**
Please include full insurance. **Prosím, započítejte plné pojištění**

CLIMATE

Prague tends to experience continental weather patterns arising from the east, but also mild, wet weather from the Atlantic. Winters are overall cold and wet, but it can stay dry and clear for long spells. When the wind blows from the north and east, it can be extremely cold. Summers are warm but rainy. June and July are two of the rainiest months of the year, while spring and autumn are changeable.

	J	F	M	A	M	J	J	A	S	O	N	D
Max												
°F	50	52	64	73	82	88	91	90	84	71	57	50
°C	10	11	18	23	28	31	33	32	29	22	14	10
Min												
°F	9	10	18	28	36	45	48	46	39	28	23	14
°C	-13	-12	-8	-2	2	7	9	8	4	-2	-5	-10

CLOTHING

Practical, casual clothing suits most occasions. In summer, bring light-weight layers but be prepared for showers, and pack a jumper in case it's cool in the evenings. In spring and autumn, a coat or thick jacket is advisable. In winter, don't forget a coat, hat and gloves. For the opera or ballet, or dinner in a fine restaurant, smart casual clothing is appropriate.

CRIME AND SAFETY

Prague is a safe, pleasant city to explore on foot. Violent crime is rare, although the number of petty scams has risen in parallel with the growing number of visitors. Stay alert on trams (especially No 22) and the metro, and in large crowds, for example on Charles Bridge or in Wenceslas Square, where pickpockets might be at work. Never change money on the streets or accept offers to break up large banknotes after withdrawing them from ATMs.

I want to report a theft **Chci ohlásit krádež**
My wallet/handbag/passport/ ticket has been stolen
Ukradli mi náprsní tašku peněženku/kabelku/pas/lístek

DRIVING

Road conditions. Road conditions in the Czech Republic are generally good. Prague itself suffers from severe congestion. Always look out for trams, slippery cobbles and tramlines, confusing one-way systems and erratic driving.

Rules and regulations. Drive on the right and overtake on the left. The speed limits are 130kmh (80mph) on motorways, 90kmh (56mph) on secondary roads and 50kmh (31mph) in built-up areas. Seat belts are compulsory. There is a zero-alcohol limit. Headlights must be kept on year-round. Children under the age of 12 are not allowed in the front seat.

Parking. Parking in the city is problematic. On-street parking is divided into zones: orange for short-term parking, green for stays of up to six hours and blue is unlimited for residents/permit-holders and for others for maximum 24 hours. Chargeable parking hours are generally Mon–Fri 8am–8pm. It is not regulated outside these hours, so it is possible to park your car free of charge then.

If you need help. Dial 1240 to call out Autoklub Bohemia Assistance, who will attempt to repair your car or take you to the nearest garage. Call 158 or 112 for the police.

Jednosměrný provoz One way
Na silnici se pracuje Roadworks
Nebezpeči Danger
Vjezd zakázán No entry
Objížďka Diversion
Pozor Caution
Pěší zóna Pedestrian zone
Vchod Entrance
Východ Exit
Full tank, please **Plnou nádrž, prosím**
petrol/diesel **benzín/nafta**
I've broken down **Mám poruchu**
There's been an accident **Stala se nehoda**
Can I park here? **Mohu zde parkovat?**

ELECTRICITY

Prague uses the 220V/50 Hz AC current, requiring standard two-pin round European plugs. Bring an adapter for UK plugs.

EMBASSIES AND CONSULATES

Ireland: Tržiště 13, Prague 1; tel: 257 011 280; www.dfa.ie/irish-embassy/czech-republic.

UK: Thunovská 14, Prague 1; tel: 257 402 111; www.gov.uk/world/organisations/british-embassy-prague.

EMERGENCIES

General emergencies: 112
Police: 158
Fire brigade: 150
Ambulance: 155

Fire! **Hoří!**
Help! **Pomoc!**
Stop thief! **Chyťte zloděje!**

GETTING THERE

By air. The national airline is ČSA (České Aeroline; www.csa.cz) but it is owned by the larger budget airline Smartwings (www.smartwings.com) which flies direct to Prague from London. Numerous budget airlines link London and regional UK airports to Prague, Brno and Pardubice. These include easyJet, (www.easyjet.com), Ryanair (www.ryanair.com), Wizz Air (www.wizzair.com) and Jet2 (www.jet2.com). British Airways (www.british airways.com) also operates flights.

By rail. Prices for rail travel are often more expensive than air travel and the journeys take longer, though can be enjoyable and are the most environmentally friendly option. Purchasing a rail pass for a set number of days can help minimise costs. Tickets can be bought at railway stations or from Czech Railways (České dráhy; www.cd.cz).

The most direct way to reach Prague from London by train is via Paris and Frankfurt, which takes around eighteen hours (for information and bookings, visit www.bahn.de). Most of the international trains arrive at the main station Praha hlavní nádraží, also known as Wilson Station, but some of them call at Smíchov.

By road. The Czech company RegioJet (www.regiojet.com) and FlixBus (www.flixbus.com) operates coaches that connect the major cities of Europe. To bring your own car you will need a valid driving licence; vehicle registration/ownership documents; a Green Card; a national identity sticker;

a first-aid kit; and a red warning triangle. To drive on motorways and some dual carriageways, you will need to buy an e-vignette online beforehand (www.edalnice.cz). These are valid for one day, ten days, a month or a year.

HEALTH AND MEDICAL CARE

Citizens of EU countries and the UK are entitled to free emergency treatment in the Czech Republic. Make sure you have your European Health Insurance Card or, for UK citizens, Global Health Insurance Card before travelling. You will be charged for any further treatment, so it still makes sense to take out adequate health and accident insurance.

A number of medical facilities with English-speaking medical personnel cater specifically to visitors. There are several foreign clinics in Prague, including Canadian Medical Care (www.canadian.cz) and Unicare Medical Center (www.unicare.cz). Prague has several large hospitals: Na Homolce, located at Roentgenova 2, Prague 5 (www.homolka.cz), has a dedicated foreigners' reception. For first aid visit Health Center Prague at Vodičkova 28–30, Prague 2 (tel: 224 220 040, www.doctor-prague.cz).

Pharmacies. For minor health problems visit a pharmacy – look for a green cross, or the word *lékárna* on the front of the shop. There are 24hr facilities at Belgická 37 (tel: 224 946 982) and Palackého 5 (tel: 224 946 982).

LANGUAGE

The national language is Czech. English is spoken in hotels but, otherwise, communication can be difficult.

The Czech alphabet has 33 letters; for instance, c and č are counted as two different letters. Here are a few tips on the pronunciation of the more difficult sounds:

ch like English **h**
ě like **ye** in *yes*
ň like the **n** in Ca*n*ute
ř like **rs** in Per*s*ian
j like **y** in *y*ellow
š like the **sh** in *sh*ine

č like **ch** in *ch*urch
c like **ts** in *ts*etse
ž like the **s** in pleasure

Do you speak English? **Mluvíte anglicky?**
I don't speak Czech **Nemluvím česky**
Good morning/Good afternoon **Dobré ráno/Dobré odpoledne**
Good evening/Good night **Dobrý večer/Dobrou noc**
Please/Thank you **Prosím/Děkuji Vám**
That's all right/You're welcome **To je v pořádku**

LGBTQ+ TRAVELLERS

LGBTQ+ travellers will generally find Prague an easy-going destination, though the queer scene is small. For up-to-date information, visit www. prague.gayguide.net; the main lesbian website (all in Czech) is www. lesba.cz.

MONEY

The Czech currency is the crown or *koruna* (Kč). Each crown is theoretically made up of 100 hellers (hal.), but they are not used. There are 5000 Kč, 2000 Kč, 1000 Kč, 500 Kč, 200 Kč and 100 Kč notes; and coins of 20 Kč, 10 Kč, 5 Kč, 2 Kč and 1 Kč.

Currency exchange. Banks open 8am–5pm. Bureaux de change often open until 10pm, but they are best avoided as they offer poor rates. There is an ATM on every street corner but avoid Euronet terminals, which charge absurd fees.

Card and phone payments. Cards and phone payments are now the norm, though you may still find some businesses that only take *hotovost* (cash).

OPENING TIMES

Banks are open 8am–5pm Monday to Friday. Bureaux de change operate daily, often until 10pm or later.

Some general shops open as early as 6am, while department stores open at 9am; both close at around 6pm, although a growing number stay open till 8pm on Thursday. Shops in the centre, particularly those aimed at tourists, often remain open until late in summer.

Museums usually open 10am–6pm and close on Sunday or Monday; exceptions include the Jewish Museum's synagogues (closed Saturday). Most galleries open 10am–6pm but close on Monday.

POLICE

There are several types of police. **State police** (tel: 158; www.policie.cz) are responsible for day-to-day policing and are armed. The best police station to contact is the one in Můstek, at Jungmannovo náměstí 9, Prague 1 (tel: 974 851 750), because there are always interpreters of several languages. **Municipal police** (tel: 156; www.mppraha.cz) are responsible for parking, crime prevention and keeping order. **Traffic police** are responsible for all road and traffic regulations. They may erect roadblocks to check documents (always carry your driving licence, passport and your car documents) or to breathalyse drivers.

POST OFFICES

If you need them, postal services (www.ceskaposta.cz) are fairly reliable for letters and postcards. Most shops that sell postcards also sell stamps, as do many hotels. Postboxes are either orange with a side slit or orange-and-blue with a front flap. The main post office (open 24hr) is at Jindříšská 909/14, just off Wenceslas Square.

PUBLIC HOLIDAYS

Government offices and banks close for the following holidays:
1 January *Nový rok* New Year's Day
1 May *Svátek práce* May Day
8 May *Vítězství nad fašismem* Victory over fascism
5 July *Slovanští věrozvěsti sv. Cyril a Metoděj* Slavic Missionaries St Cyril and St Methodius

6 July *Výročí úmrtí Jana Husa* Jan Hus's death

28 September *Den české státnosti* Day of the Czech Statehood

28 October *První československá republika* First Czechoslovak Republic

17 November *Den boje za svobodu a demokracii* Day of Struggle for Liberty and Democracy

24 December *Štědrý den* Christmas Eve

25/26 December *Vánoční svátky* Christmas/Boxing Day

Movable date *Velikonoční pondělí* Easter Monday

TELEPHONES

Most phone numbers consist of nine digits, including the area code. You should dial the entire nine-digit number even if you are dialling within the same area code.

The international code for the Czech Republic is +420. The city code for Prague is 2, but this is included in the nine-digit number.

To make an international call dial 00 or (+), then the country code, then the number.

Most international mobile phones will work in Prague. However, for longer stays it is much cheaper to buy one of the easily available local pay-as-you-go SIM cards. The main companies are O2 (www.cz.o2.com), T-Mobile (www.t-mobile.cz) and Vodafone (www.vodafone.cz).

TIME ZONES

Prague operates on Central European Time (CET). This is one hour ahead of GMT in winter and two hours ahead of GMT in summer.

TIPPING

Tipping is appreciated but levels are low (it is enough to round up the bill, or to leave the change).

TOILETS

There are public toilets at some metro stations and in shopping centres. There is usually a small fee of around 10–20 Kč.

If there are no man or woman symbols to help you, ladies' toilets will be labelled *Ženy* or *Dámy*, mens' will be *Muži* or *Páni*.

TOURIST INFORMATION

Visit the **CzechTourism** website for information on Prague and the whole Czech Republic (www.czechtourism.com). The **Czech Tourist Authority**'s information centre in Prague is at Vinohradska 46. **Prague City Tourism** (www.prague.eu) information centres can be found at the Old Town Hall, Staroměstské náměstí 1, Prague 1, Rytířska 31, Prague 1, and Wenceslas Square, Prague 1. There are also many commercial agencies offering tourist information and selling tours.

TRANSPORT

Prague has one of the best public-transport systems in the world (www. dpp.cz). Tickets and passes can be used on all forms of transport. Each ticket has a time limit, and you pay more for a longer limit. The cheapest ticket costs 30Kč and allows either thirty minutes of travel with no transfer or five stops on the metro with no line change. A 40Kč ticket allows ninety minutes of travel and allows line change or tram transfer within that time. There are also very good value 24hr tickets (120Kč) and 72hr passes (320Kč). Children up to 15 years and people over 70 travel free of charge.

Tickets can be bought at metro stations (there are automatic ticket machines which give instructions in English and supply change) and newsstands. They must be validated in the small yellow machines before you catch the tram or arrive at the metro. However, most people now use the public transport app Lítačka on their smartphone.

Buses and trams. Buses, which are clean and punctual, tend to provide a service out to the Prague suburbs rather than compete with trams in the city. A comprehensive network of tram routes connects both sides of the river. Each stop shows the tram number passing there and a timetable. Most city maps show the tram routes in addition to the location of the major attractions. All trams run from 4.30am–midnight, but several routes are also designated as night services (24hr). Purchase your ticket before you travel and validate it as you enter, unless you are transferring from another tram or metro within your allotted time.

Metro. The extremely efficient Prague metro opened in 1974 and provides a great service for visitors. There are three interlinked lines, and metro maps can be found at each station. Metro signs above ground feature a stylised M incorporated into an arrow pointing downwards. The metro operates from around 5am–midnight.

Taxis. Taxis are main source of complaints from visitors to the city. Wild overcharging of foreigners is still a problem. Always use public transport if possible. From the airport you must now use Uber. If you absolutely must travel by taxi, have your hotel or the tourist office call you one.

Where do I get the bus to the city centre/airport? **Odkud jede autobus do centra města?/na letiště?**
Take these bags to the bus/taxi, please **Prosím, odneste tato zavazadla k autobusu/taxi**

VISAS AND ENTRY REQUIREMENTS

Passports/visas. Citizens of the EU need only a passport to visit the Czech Republic for up to 180 days. UK citizens can stay ninety days.

Customs. It is illegal to export antiques without a permit.

Index

THE **MINI** ROUGH GUIDE TO
PRAGUE

First Edition 2025

Editor: Joanna Reeves
Author: Lindsay Bennett
Updater: Marc Di Duca
Picture Manager: Tom Smyth
Cartography Update: Katie Bennett
Production Operations Manager: Katie Bennett
Publishing Technology Manager: Rebeka Davies
Head of Publishing: Sarah Clark
Photography Credits: 123RF 76, 78, 90, 92; Apa
Publications 74, 117; Bigstock 96; iStcok 29, 43,
49, 53, 54, 56, 60, 62, 64, 73, 94, 100, 107, 108, 113;
iStock 16ML, 45, 67; Národní divadlo 14MC, 27;
Public domain 99; Rod Purcell/Apa Publications
44, 46, 47, 51, 58, 70, 81, 87, 89, 101, 102, 103, 104,
110, 114; Shutterstock 1, 4, 5, 7, 9, 10, 13, 14MC,
14TC, 14ML, 14TL, 14TL, 15, 15T, 15M, 15M, 16TL,
16ML, 16MC, 18TL, 18ML, 18MC, 20TL, 20ML,
20MC, 20ML, 23, 25, 30, 32, 34, 37, 40, 68, 75, 82,
84, 93, 118; ŠJů 18ML
Cover Credits: Church of Our Lady before Týn
Shutterstock

About the author

Marc Di Duca has been a travel guide author
for twenty years and has contributed to over
150 guides for major travel publishers. He has
covered destinations as diverse as Siberia and
the Caribbean but is based in the beautiful spa
town of Mariánské Lázně in the Czech Republic
where he lives with his Ukrainian wife Tanya and
their two sons.

Distribution

UK, Ireland and Europe: Apa Publications (UK)
Ltd; sales@roughguides.com
United States and Canada: Ingram Publisher
Services; ips@ingramcontent.com
Australia and New Zealand: Booktopia;
retailer@booktopia.com.au
Worldwide: Apa Publications (UK) Ltd;
sales@roughguides.com

Special Sales, Content Licensing
and CoPublishing

Rough Guides can be purchased in bulk
quantities at discounted prices. We can create
special editions, personalised jackets and
corporate imprints tailored to your needs.
sales@roughguides.com; http://roughguides.com

Contact us

Every effort has been made to provide accurate
information in this publication, but changes
are inevitable. The publisher cannot be held
responsible for any resulting loss, inconvenience
or injury sustained by any traveller as a result
of information or advice contained in the
guide. We would appreciate it if readers would
call our attention to any errors or outdated
information, or if you feel we've left something
out. Please send your comments with the
subject line 'Rough Guide Mini Prague Update' to
mail@uk.roughguides.com.

Prague Metro

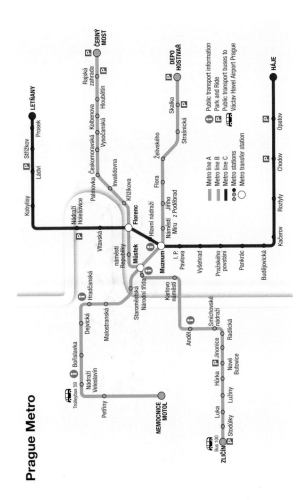